Embracing Life On Our Own Terms

Dr Angela C. Robertson

Embracing Life On Our Own Terms

Paradise Publishing 2021

Disclaimer: This collection of personal stories was written in consultation with the individuals concerned and is published with their consent. The contents are the personal views of each individual and as such the author and publisher disclaim any liability in connection with the use of this information or for issues of fact or interpretation. Neither the author, nor the publisher accept referral fees or commissions from individuals or companies that may be mentioned in this publication.

ISBN: 978-0-9951371-3-4

Cover Image:

Steven Novak   Novakillustrations.com

Books by the same author
in the *'Older and Bolder'* series

Life On Our Own Terms

ISBN: 978-0-473-50082-5 Paperback

Celebrating Life On Our Own Terms

ISBN: 978-0-473-51912-4 Paperback

CONTENTS

"The moment in between what you once were, and who you are now becoming, is where the dance of life really takes place".

Barbara De Angelis

PREFACE

With our extended lifespans, the world is changing, and so too has our perspective on ageing. As life is a continuous adventure, our chronological age becomes less and less relevant. Later life offers so many possibilities for personal growth and the opportunity to channel our time and energy into the activities we enjoy and the relationships that really matter. A huge debt of gratitude is due to the awesome individuals, from diverse backgrounds and all walks of life, who generously shared their stories with me. With their permission a lifetime of wildly different experiences has been condensed into this collection of short cameo stories. This is no mean feat as the men and women featured in this book range in age from their mid-50's to 100 years! They all live in New Zealand for at least part of the year and have all reached a stage in life where it is possible to look both back and forward. As a result, they are mindfully aware of their unique experience, the people they have met along the way who have influenced who they are today, and the choices they have made that will shape their future. It's a privilege to be able to share their stories with you. These individuals are embracing life on their own terms, and inspired by their example, whatever our age and circumstances, so can we!

"Ageing is not lost youth, but a new stage of opportunity and strength".

Betty Friedan

INTRODUCTION

Population ageing is a global phenomenon. Virtually every country in the world is experiencing growth in the size and proportion of people aged 65 and over. It is predicted that one in six people will be over 65 years of age by 2050, up from one in eleven in 2019, (World Population Ageing 2019: Highlights (un.org)). In New Zealand, it's expected a fifth of the population will be over the age of 65 by 2034, (Better Later Life He Oranga Kaumātua 2019 to 2034 (msd.govt.nz)). Although there is no way of knowing how long we are going to live, and accepting that we all age differently, with increased life expectancy and dramatic improvements in health care, there is a good chance many of us will live for a lot longer than our predecessors. Looking ahead, to what we may traditionally call 'retirement', we may have potentially only lived for two-thirds of our lives. Given the gift of healthier extended lifespans, it makes sense to embrace the ageing process, take good care of ourselves, enjoy life's pleasures, and make the most of the additional years later life offers.

For many, mid-life is a time for reflection. It's one of those phases in life when we take stock of what we've experienced to date, what we've achieved, and who and what is important to us. In the midst of the COVID pandemic, we are even more mindful of what has gone before, acutely aware of the present, and speculate about the future. While the second half of life is an opportunity to re-vision and re-ignite our lives, we can change gears at any age if we choose to. After all, our chronological age is just a number, and many believe it's a state of mind.   To paraphrase what King Solomon and Buddha both said, 'what we think, we are' – we create our reality.

What thoughts come to mind when you think ahead? Are you looking forward with excitement or apprehension?

Believing that a) life is full of possibilities, and b) we learn from other people's experience, I began an incredible journey of my own. I randomly asked men and women over the age of 50, from all walks of life, to share their stories with me, and where possible did this in exchange for a pot of my home-made jam. During our conversations I captured the context of their earlier lives, their aspirations, plans, and perspectives, their resilience in the face of adversity, and documented the choices they made that shaped their future. These individuals demonstrate that, depending on one's mindset, whatever their age and circumstances, later life has the potential to be even more fulfilling than what has gone before. It's a privilege to share their cameo stories with you in this third book in the 'Older and Bolder' series. These individuals are embracing life on their own terms, and without exception they are making the most what life has to offer.

Let me introduce you to them.

PHIL BYRNE

Phil, the youngest of four boys, was born in Reading a large historic market town in Berkshire, England. His father was a teacher at Sonning Common School and the family lived in one of the Nissen huts that were erected in the school grounds for the War. In the mid 1970's, when Phil was 11 years old, the family moved to Chester where he attended Christleton High School, a large secondary modern school located in a village on the outskirts of town. In those days there were 45 or more students in each class, and although Phil recalls enjoying school, he found it easy to act out, misbehave and have fun in the overcrowded classroom. When he was 16 years old, labelled a troublemaker he was encouraged to leave school and join the military, a career path his three elder brothers had also chosen.

In 1982, Phil and his mate Jim Short applied and were accepted as boy sailors in the Royal Navy. Looking back Phil said, "military training provided strict guidelines and structure to life, instilled a sense of pride and offered adventure" – all the things he needed as a teenager. He had joined the Navy in the months leading up to the Falklands War in 1982. When the war broke out, he volunteered to go on this big adventure, but his request was denied as he was too young and still under training.

Phil was posted to the Royal Naval Air Station Culdrose in Cornwall, one of the largest helicopter bases in Europe, where he trained as an aircraft engineer. At this base, aircraft were prepped to be shipped out to the Falklands. During this period several of Phil's mates died when the SS Atlantic Conveyor carrying helicopters and supplies was struck by Exocet missiles on the 25th May 1982. Later Phil made several trips to Ascension Island and all the way down to the Falklands to test ship missile systems with a fleet target group. It was an incredibly dangerous place to be as Phil said the area had been "heavily mined by the Argentinians" and remained so for years after the war was over.

Phil loved military life and the opportunities it provided. In 1983, as part of a task group, he had the opportunity to sail around the world on HMS Invincible, a light aircraft carrier used by the Royal Navy. The ship was docked in Wellington for five days and this is where Phil met Lisa, who was to become his future wife. When Phil returned to Portland Naval Base in Weymouth, Lisa moved to the UK so they could be together. The couple married in the late 1980's. In 1990 Phil joined the Commando Squadron and became a member of '3 Commando Brigade'– widely recognised as the UK's 'Tip of the Spear' and usually the first troops into any combat zone. Once trained he undertook multiple tours of duty in Northern Ireland, Sierra Leone and was involved in the Gulf War - a war waged by a coalition of forces from 35 nations.

After nearly 25 years in the Navy, promoted to Senior Trade Chief in the Commando Circuit, Phil also completed a degree and was offered a commission, but he turned it down, as he and his wife had always planned to return to New Zealand when he turned 40 years of age.

In 2004, the couple and their young son Sam came back to New Zealand and settled in the Manawatū where Lisa's family lived. Phil immediately sought work, but these were tough times, and few organisations were looking for staff. Phil, being highly motivated, was prepared to do anything rather than be idle so he knocked on doors and offered to volunteer his services. Fieldair Engineering Ltd initially took him on to sweep the hanger floor, but it became clear that Phil was not only easy to get along with - he was also highly motivated and always looking for ways to make himself useful in the industry. A couple of months later, when one of the Managers left Fieldair, Phil applied for the job. The senior managers on the interview panel were amazed when they saw his curriculum vitae and learned about Phil's qualifications, skills and experience. Following an interview, Phil was offered the job. He said, "I grew in the role", and so did the team he managed. It wasn't long before Phil took on the responsibility for managing additional departments at Fieldair, and over the four years he worked there, the company made a substantial profit.

Phil's career went from strength to strength. He became widely known in the aviation industry in New Zealand and was head-hunted by other organisations to work for them. In 2006 he was persuaded to take on the challenging role as Engineering Manager at Airwork Ltd in Auckland with the responsibility for 150 staff located across five bases. By this time Phil and his wife had parted ways, so a new role in a different location was very appealing. Whilst he enjoyed his time with Airwork Ltd immensely, he was enticed back to Fieldair in the Manawatū in 2007 to take on a senior management role with considerable responsibility. Five years later, the Chief Executive of Hawker

Pacific offered Phil a job in Australia, managing their operation in Cairns and Sydney. It was a fantastic opportunity. Phil and his partner Kay moved to Trinity Park in Northern Queensland where he bought an apartment, and he became absorbed in his full-on job in the aviation industry in Australia for the next three years.

In 2019, Phil returned to New Zealand. At 55 years of age, having worked with aviation companies all his life, he felt that it was time to do something different. Phil was keen to start a business, but he also wanted a more balanced lifestyle which enabled him to spend more time with his fantastic new partner Kay and their families. The couple bought a property on the Kāpiti Coast and, as they were settling into their new home, they mulled over their ideas to start a business. The 'aha' moment came when a local retailer delivered a new fridge to their home. Phil watched as the delivery vehicle reversed into his driveway puffing great clouds of smoke. Phil helped the guy unload the new fridge and then watched as the vehicle drove away in another great plume of smoke - leaving behind a big puddle of oil in his driveway! It wasn't the first time he had witnessed this scenario. Phil had always been concerned about the environment. He knew he could offer a quality eco-friendly delivery service, and what's more, he could pick up and make deliveries at a time that suited the customer, rather than the time that worked for the supplier. He had all the skills – a regular at the gym he was physically fit and healthy, self-motivated, liked people and was willing to help them, and he wanted to do what he could to reduce the carbon footprint. The idea for Phil's business was to establish a fast, reliable, cost-effective, environmentally friendly pick-up and delivery service.

After researching his business idea, 'Eco Shifter' was formed and within a few short months his first fully electric delivery vehicle was providing a 24/7 service for customers across the Wellington, Kāpiti and Horowhenua regions www.ecoshifter.nz

Phil made a successful mid-life career transition and loves working in his business. The nature of the work "keeps me fit and healthy, I have the freedom to work hours that work for me and my customers, I get to help people every day offering an efficient environmentally friendly service, and I'm having fun". As Phil is an engineer by trade, he is able to think of innovative ways on how to move things safely for his clients. Eco Shifter clearly provides a much-needed service for the community as Phil often gets repeat business from his customers which, he says, "is very satisfying". The business is growing so fast that Phil has been able to employ others to help him on an 'as needs' basis. Looking ahead, Phil is considering franchising as a way of expanding his business in other locations around New Zealand.

Now that Phil is self-employed, he has found more time to undertake voluntary work. A keen cyclist, he repairs bicycles for under privileged children in a Te Horo workshop coordinated by Energise Ōtaki Bike Space. The project reconditions bikes that are donated to them and "encourages children to get off their tablets, get energised, bike to school, and enjoy the outdoors". Phil teaches youngsters how to maintain and ride their bicycles and gives away free cycle helmets.

Phil is also the pilot cyclist on a tandem for a blind member of the community. Taking his health and wellbeing seriously Phil is a regular at the gym focusing on weights and cardiovascular training. He also rides his bike regularly and enjoys running. Given these lifestyle changes, Phil now has more time to spend with his partner Kay and their family and friends.

Reflecting on his story it was interesting to note that Phil's siblings, all of whom now live in the UK, were drawn to a career in the military. All three of his brothers joined the Royal Air Force (RAF) in various trades, and one moved onto a successful career in the Special Air Services (SAS), so Phil was unique in joining the Royal Navy and the Commandos. They all found it to be a rewarding career, and his parents were always thrilled to tell their friends that between their boys they had provided over 100 years' service to Her Majesty. Sam, Phil's adult son also chose a career path with the military. Sam serves with the Royal New Zealand Air Force (RNZAF) and is based at Ōhakea.

The following quotes, both courtesy of Winston Churchill, resonate with Phil

"Success is the ability to go from one failure to another with no loss of enthusiasm."

"Success is not final, failure is not fatal, it is the courage to continue that counts."

In essence Phil says, "never give up and never stop trying".

Phil Byrne, boy sailor in the Royal Navy

Phil is on the far right in the front row with 846 Sqdn.
The photo was taken in Belfast during the troubles.
The aircraft is a Sea King Mk4.

Phil on the far left back row, with his colleagues at a missile testing site in South Wales where they generally tested both Seadart and Seawolf missile systems in the late 1980's.

This photo of Phil was taken in one of the jungle clearings in Sierra Leone that was used to resupply SAS and Commando forces during the 2000 intervention by British forces. The aircraft is a Sea King Mk4.

Phil with his fully electric 'Eco-Shifter' delivery vehicle

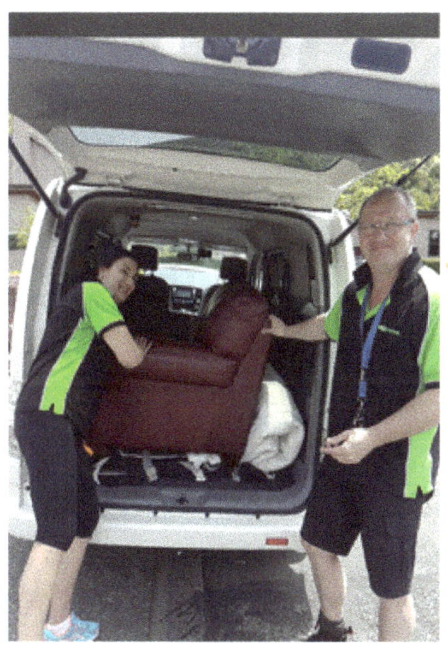

Phil gets to help people every day offering an efficient friendly service.

DIANE WHITE

Diane, the eldest of six children was born and raised on a rural farm in Waipati, Southland. Her father became a farmer when provision was made to finance ex-servicemen with low rates of interest rehabilitation loans, a scheme that helped people re-establish themselves in civilian life. Her mother was a stay-at-home Mum, and she has memories of a 'pretty idyllic upbringing'. Diane and her siblings attended the local two-teacher primary school, and the local community hall was the hub for the community's social activities. As an adolescent, leaving this family centred rural community, to become a weekly boarder (Sunday-Friday) at St Catherine's School for Girls in Invercargill was a bit of a culture shock for Diane. At St Catherine's the girls were taught by Dominican nuns. As the daily regimes were different to what she had been accustomed to at primary school, she missed her family. Although Diane struggled to adjust at first, over the four years she spent at Saint Catherine's she grew to love it and thrived in this environment. She did well academically, enjoyed music and the arts, took part in sporting activities including netball and athletics, and made lasting friendships. After passing School Certificate and the University Entrance examination, Diane left school in 1968.

In the late 1960's securing a government job was a very attractive option for women. The pay scales were good in comparison with traditional roles for women at the time (e.g., teaching, and nursing) and New Zealand's benefits and welfare services were progressively expanding, thus providing young women new career paths. As a young woman Diane was looking forward to a bit of excitement and a social life. When she left school, she decided to stay in Invercargill, where she secured a job with the government, and started dating. Before long Diane found she was pregnant. Naturally, she was distressed about her predicament and when she told her parents the news, they were heart broken. In those days there was no financial support for single parents, so her options were limited to; have the baby adopted or marry the father of the child. Although meetings with adoption agencies commenced, this wasn't the preferred option. Under pressure from her boyfriend's parents the young couple got married.

Diane was 18 years old when their first child was born in August 1969. The family expanded when several children were born in quick succession. Times were tough raising a big family on a truck driver's income, but with support from their families, who helped them out with meat, groceries and knitted clothes, they made ends meet. During this frugal time Diane became quite proficient in sewing and knitting, which she said she can hardly believe when she looks at the family photos. Although the couple tried to make the best of their marriage, they grew apart and eventually went their separate ways in 1979.

Diane describes her children as being "the light of my life". Raising the children as a single parent, (three of them were under four at the time), she took on cleaning jobs and worked as a grill cook at night to support the family, rather than live on the Domestic Purposes Benefit that was offered to solo parents. Diane met new friends at the grill, one of whom was the chef, who she started dating. Before long they became a couple, and they had a child of their own in 1981.

Diane and her partner bought and managed a catering business, which they operated for the next 25 years. In the late 1980's Diane's father was the President of Gore's Returned Services Association (RSA) Club. To increase the Club's revenue, a bistro was established in the RSA. For 12 years, Diane managed the bistro as part of their catering business, as well as preparing the catering for all manner of functions, such as weddings and other celebrations.

Sadly, a series of tragedies struck during this period of Diane's life, reinforcing the fragility of family life and how this can change in a heartbeat. First her younger brother died in a trail bike accident in 1986, aged 25 years. Recalling this horrendous event Diane said it brought her and her siblings together in a different and closer way than they were before, "never taking our lives and blessings for granted". Both of Diane's much-loved parents passed away at a fairly young age, and within a couple of years of one another. Her mother died suddenly in 1995, aged 66. This came as a huge shock to the family as she had no obvious health issues. Her father died in 1997, aged 80. Then in 2000, Diane's niece and goddaughter, was killed in a car accident a month before her 16th birthday. This was her sister's only daughter so one can barely imagine how Diane would have felt with four daughters of her own. Once again, all of the siblings gathered as one to support her sister's family. Reflecting on these poignant incidents Diane said they have been truly defining times in her life.

As time passed Diane's children grew up, and with more time to herself, she had a hankering to study. Initially she enrolled in an accounting course on a part-time basis to assist in the management of their business. Gradually, as her appetite for learning and development grew, she undertook papers in other disciplines including, feminist perspectives, business studies, communication, effective listening, facilitation and courses in personal growth. This occurred in the days before personal computers, so all of her assignments were done by hand.

The turning point came when Diane took a paper in children's issues, which she pursued with a passion. As a result, she was accepted to complete a Diploma in Social Work and she chipped away at it to achieve the qualification while managing her job working at the grill. In April 2000, a friend who was a Social Worker, helped her to get a placement at Child Youth and Family. This gave Diane the opportunity to gain practical on-the-job experience in the government agency that provides services for vulnerable children, young offenders and their families. It also provided her with financial support while she studied. Diane completed her qualification and graduated in 2006, but the achievement was tinged with sadness. Through her commitment to her studies over the years Diane had grown both personally and professionally, and she had discovered her vocation. The years of study and working in shift work in two different hospitality businesses took their toll on the relationship with her partner. After living and working together for 25 years, the relationship came to an end. It was time for them both to go their separate ways.

Diane really enjoyed her work, and, following her graduation, she remained in her full-time role with the Department of Child Youth and Family Services in Gore and set up a home on her own. Reflecting on this experience Diane said, "I developed a bigger and deeper appreciation for so many things – life isn't always fair. Sometimes it doesn't work out for people". Working on a day-to-day basis with people who were struggling to cope, it bothered her that some people who had an easier road could think differently and didn't really understand the social and economic issues facing some families. It's a conundrum. In her role Diane gained lots of insight into how the world works for some of her clients. She also developed a broader awareness of the powerful influence that social media has on people's lives more generally, whereby people generally accept what they are told rather than learn the facts before making judgements about others in the community.

In 2009, Diane travelled overseas with her brother and sister-in-law to visit family in the United Kingdom. While there she took the opportunity to tour around the country taking in the sights and also visited Ireland. A couple of years later in 2013, one of Diane's friends asked her to accompany her on a trip to Kylemore Abbey Estate in Connemara, which is about an hour's drive from Galway in the west of Ireland. Kylemore Abbey is a Benedictine monastery in the grounds of Kylemore Castle. Over the years the Benedictine nuns have restored the Abbey's gardens and the church. They opened the Abbey and grounds and the six-acre walled Victorian gardens to the public and offered academic programmes and retreats. The self-sustaining Estate is a very special place. It's a working monastery run by the Benedictine community and is one of the biggest tourist attractions in the west of Ireland. Visiting Kylemore Abbey where she worked as a volunteer with the Benedictine community, was another defining experience for Diane. "It was uplifting, restorative and peaceful". It was easy for her to develop an affinity for this awe-inspiring place and the encounter with the nuns reconnected her to her spiritual roots.

Since that first visit to Kylemore Abbey, Diane has been returning to the Estate every year for the past seven years to work as a volunteer – doing whatever tasks need doing - making soap, or chocolate, cleaning and working in the commercial garden. While she is there, she lives in shared accommodation on the Estate with students from all over the world. While Diane appreciates this experience isn't for everyone, she feels 'very privileged to be a member of the Benedictine community'.

During these years Diane continued her work with Child Youth and Family, a position she held for 17 years. In 2017, the dynamics in her team changed and this had a huge impact on the people who worked there. Disillusioned, retirement seemed the best option at the time. Had the situation been different, she would never have considered retiring. Nevertheless, with more time available to her, and being a people person at heart, Diane volunteered with Hospice Southland, an organisation that provides specialist palliative care for those with life-limiting illness. She worked in the Gore Hospice shop that sells donated goods to help support the running cost of the hospice services. Diane enjoyed the work. She said, "it was lovely to see former clients who were so amicable", and they were pleased to see her again too.

While working at the Hospice, a representative from St John's told her that they were looking for a person to lead 'Friends of the Hospital' – a group of volunteers that work four-hour shifts supporting patients and their families in the hospital environment. The role appealed to Diane, so she applied for the advertised position and got the job. In this role she was responsible for organising the roster and managing the induction programme for the volunteers at Gore Hospital. When the hospital's Social Worker was due to have surgery, Diane was asked if she would fill in for him in his absence, and she agreed to do so. Following the handover process, she was once again working as a Social Worker on a full-time basis, which she really enjoyed. When the incumbent returned to his substantive role in a part-time capacity following his surgery, Diane was offered a part-time permanent position at Gore Hospital, an arrangement that works well for everyone to this day.

She also works as a Needs Assessor for the Ministry of Health working with clients in Rest Homes and hospital care units ensuring they receive the support they need. Social work has been both a challenging and rewarding career for Diane, one in which she has been able to draw on her own personal experience and facilitate with competence and compassion.

As previously noted, Diane's family is an integral part of her life and brings her so much joy. In semi-retirement, Diane lives a purposeful life. Prior to the COVID outbreak she divided her time between her family and her paid and voluntary work in New Zealand, and the Benedictine community at Kylemore Abbey in Ireland. Diane said, "it has been and continues to be a fascinating and incredible journey, connecting with so many lives along the way". At the time of writing, she has 15 grandchildren, two step grandchildren and three great grandchildren – all but two of whom live in New Zealand.

Leo F. Buscaglia's reflections on life and the afterlife is quite pertinent. He said,

"Ancient Egyptians believed that upon death they would be asked two questions and their answers would determine whether they could continue their journey in the afterlife. The first question was, 'Did you bring joy?' The second was, 'Did you find joy?"

This quote by Terry Orlick also resonates,

"The heart of human excellence often begins to beat when you discover a pursuit that absorbs you, frees you, challenges you, or gives you a sense of meaning, joy, or passion."

Kylemore Castle

Diane at Kylemore Abbey

Diane, second from the left in the back row,
with some of the nuns and volunteers at Kylemore Abbey

Diane While

Diane's children are "the light of my life"

Diane's family bring her so much joy

Diane White

PAUL ANDERSON

Dr Paul Anderson is a specialist surgeon and lecturer who runs a free Specialist Review Clinic in Kawerau in the Bay of Plenty, in the North Island of New Zealand. This clinic is the first of its kind in New Zealand, allowing him to see patients for whom GPs are concerned, given the time it may take for them to be seen and treated in the public system. Paul reviews the patients in order to help prioritise their treatment. He lectures part of the week in anatomy/physiology and clinical sciences, in the Department of Nursing at the indigenous Ngāti Awa Wānanga /Awanuiārangi in Whakatāne. He is also the founder of Specialists without Borders, a non-profit organisation that takes high quality medical education through volunteer specialists, into developing countries, such as Rwanda, Malawi and Zimbabwe.

Paul started life in Ōpōtiki, where his grandfather George Anderson drove model T Fords up through the Motu Gorge, to collect goods and services from Gisborne. His parents relocated to Rotorua when he was five, which is where he developed a love for sports, especially rugby, going on to represent New Zealand Universities and later becoming a junior All Black and an All-Black trialist. Although he was a keen student, winning the history prize at school, Paul admits he was "a rebellious teenager", which initially impacted on his academic abilities. At 16 years of age, he was asked to leave home by his father. Forced to become self-reliant, he headed to Hamilton to attend Waikato University and Hamilton Teachers College. There he embarked on what was to become a life-long learning journey and an educational career path spanning four continents.

While Paul began his tertiary education in the Waikato, he always had the feeling that he wanted to study medicine. He realises now that he needed to deal with all the rebellious issues first. Finding his way in Hamilton with new friends helped him on that journey of developing responsibility, and he became the youngest captain at the time for the Waikato provincial rugby team. Paul thinks this helped lead him back to his original ambition of studying medicine. Researching ways to achieve his innate goal, he discovered a curriculum in Glasgow, which covered anatomy, physiology, pathology, psychology and kinesiology. The chance to see another country and the nature of the curriculum appealed to him, so he shifted first to London, and then subsequently to Glasgow to complete this qualification. Paul found the course so stimulating, it ignited his interest for more. When he was offered a bursary to complete a master's degree at the University of California, he accepted in a flash. He graduated with a double major in sports medicine and sports sociology, while also lecturing to undergraduates and teaching children to swim to help pay his way. Shortly after graduating, a visiting professor from Stellenbosch University in the Western Cape province of South Africa, offered Paul an inaugural scholarship to complete a PhD in sports medicine/sports science. It was an incredible opportunity, one which Paul quickly accepted.

In 1978 when Paul arrived in South Africa, the apartheid political and social system was in place. The White population ruled the country, and segregation from the Black population was legislated and legally enforced. South Africans were divided by their race, and the different races were forced to live separately from each other. Essentially what he found was the Black population in townships and the White population in the cities and rural areas. For Paul, who had grown up in a multicultural society in New Zealand, it was a huge culture shock as he was suddenly confronted by a racially segregated society. Shocked by the nature of segregation, which was apartheid, he struggled to pursue his research in sports medicine, which resulted in a bold decision - to write a thesis and let the world know about the inequities of racial discrimination. With the support of his American PhD supervisor, Paul changed his thesis topic from sports medicine to one on, 'Politics Race and Sport in South Africa'. This was an extremely challenging topic, especially given the university was Afrikaans speaking and actively supported legislated segregation. Understandably his research journey, was fraught with numerous challenges, including being put under surveillance by the notorious Bureau of State Security. His phone was tapped, his apartment checked out and it appeared initially that he would have to leave the country to have his PhD published. Nonetheless, after much international discussion, two years later he defended his thesis, and was awarded his PhD with distinction. This was recognised internationally as an amazing academic achievement given the political climate.

Paul had planned to return to the United States following the completion of his thesis to take up a lecturing position. However, a couple of weeks before he was due to leave South Africa, there was an encounter with the Deputy Vice Chancellor of the University of Cape Town at a barbecue. He encouraged Paul to follow his first love and study medicine at the University of Cape Town, insisting they would give him credit for all the study he had done. The University was associated with Groote Schuur Hospital, where the first heart transplant by Dr Christian Barnard had taken place in 1987, and the University had defied apartheid by taking in black students. It didn't take Paul long to make up his mind, as he had always known he wanted to do medicine. When he discussed it with his mother and father, they said they would help where they could, as it was an opportunity that couldn't be refused, especially as the University of Cape Town medical school was ranked amongst the top medical schools in the world. The only issue for Paul was that as a foreign resident, he needed to find the money to study medicine and to live. Paul remembers being down to his last few cents at the time, wondering whether he would have to forgo medicine and return to New Zealand, when he suddenly obtained a part-time job with the South African Eye Bank Foundation. The Foundation employed Paul to remove eyes from homicide victims at the local police mortuary. Paul said he would "take the eyes from the homicide victims, then remove the corneas in a small laboratory, after which they would be sent around Africa to be used as corneal transplants". It was a lifeline which paid for his university education and provided many stories for his future novels.

Paul has good memories of doing medicine in South Africa, describing it as (other than the segregation), "a rare privilege. Not only was the medical teaching superb, but the exposure to real life pathology was unparalleled, and the extremes of medicine were exciting and challenging".

In his final year Paul met a surgical registrar who later that year became his wife. As newly-weds Paul and Margaret relocated to the Waikato in New Zealand, where Paul completed his internship. By that time, he also knew that he wanted to specialise in surgery. Completing his internship, he sat and passed the FRCS, through the Royal College of Surgeons in Edinburgh, the professional qualification to practice as a surgeon.

With his wife Margaret, who was one of the first female surgical trainees in New Zealand, the couple moved to Auckland as part of their surgical training. Three years later Margaret qualified as a consultant surgeon and was offered a position in Dunedin, where Paul continued his surgical training as a registrar. The work was extremely demanding with both doing surgery and long hours. Margaret became pregnant and indicated to Paul that she was going to return to her family in South Africa, so Paul applied for permission to complete his final year of surgical supervision in Cape Town. His request was granted "as long as I kept a logbook of surgeries I had undertaken and submitted it to the New Zealand surgical committee every three months".

Back in Cape Town, Paul was appointed as a vascular registrar. As it was so busy in surgery, he was on call every second night of the week. When he sent his logbook to the New Zealand College of Surgeons, they were astounded by the number of operations he had completed in three months, almost the equivalent of nine months in New Zealand. In January 1992, after the birth of his son Jordan, Paul returned briefly to New Zealand to complete the fellowship exam for the Royal Australasian College of Surgeons (RACS), which allowed him to return to a junior consultant post in surgery in Cape Town.

One Sunday evening in 1993 needing to get out, Paul remembered one of his patients telling him about the fabulous singing in a multiracial church auditorium. Deciding to go and visit St James's Church he was sitting in the auditorium, listening to a beautiful rendition of Ave Maria, when suddenly a masked gunman in a camouflage uniform brandishing an AK-47 entered a side door. As he advanced towards the congregation, the masked gunman shot the young girl on the stage, who had been singing. Three other gunmen similarly dressed were behind the first, and they began firing their weapons at the congregation and throwing grenades indiscriminately. Many people were killed and maimed creating a traumatic nightmare for the people involved. Paul sustained significant injuries to an arm and one of his feet, multiple injuries from the grenade fragments, and a ruptured eardrum. He spent hours in surgery where colleagues and friends worked hard to repair the damage, so that Paul could potentially continue his surgical career. He spent months recovering from his physical injuries and then had to deal with post-traumatic stress. Paul said, "Post-Traumatic Stress Disorder (PTSD) was not well-defined at that time, the advice being basically that you survived and got on with life".

Unable to deal with the flashbacks and nightmares Paul decided to write about the horrific experience. Finding the process of writing about the terror attack extremely cathartic, he showed the story to others who suggested making the story into a novel. He later turned his story into a medical thriller called 'Does It Hurt To Die' (published by Austin Macauley in 2012). Little did he know at the time that his book would find its way to Hollywood, be converted into a screenplay, and attract the interest of Russell Crowe and then Angelina Jolie.

During his recovery period, Paul visited friends in Hong Kong, and while there attended a surgical conference where he met Jim Toouli, the Professor of Surgery from Flinders University in Adelaide South Australia. Jim, who is an international expert in hepatobiliary surgery, (liver, pancreas, gall bladder and bile duct), shared news about a liver transplant programme that was about to start at Flinders. Paul chatted to him about his involvement with the liver transplant programme in Cape Town, after which Jim suggested he applied for a job at Flinders University. It was a great opportunity to be involved in the development of a liver transplant programme and the timing, following the terrorist attack, was perfect.

Paul was initially appointed as a Senior Surgical Registrar at Flinders in Adelaide where his surgical career flourished. Over the next few years, learning with and from highly regarded experts in the field, he became the locum professor of surgery for a short time, while he also developed an interest in bariatric surgery. He was then sent to Belgium to learn keyhole weight loss surgery. When Paul returned, he established one of the first three laparoscopic/keyhole weight loss surgical clinics in Australia.

Such was the demand, Paul received patient referrals from all over Australia, and became more and more busy. As a result, Paul and his wife Margaret separated. The only positive thing Paul recalls about this separation is that he became a single parent, which required him "to work less to look after my favourite son Jordan".

In 2005, more than a decade after the terrorist attack, Paul was asked to lead a medical team to Rwanda, as part of a world-wide response to mark the 10th anniversary of the Rwandan genocide. This was to be part of the world's apology, for not having prevented the genocide. Given Paul's awful experience with terrorism in Africa, he was at first very hesitant to return, but he said, "part of me felt guilty about having trained in Africa and I wanted to contribute or give something back for what they had given me in medicine". Paul subsequently led an international team to a hospital in Gisenyi, close to the Rwanda/Congo border, where they performed surgery for two weeks. The group also comprised nurses, physiotherapists, occupational therapists, a hospital administrator and a pharmacist, all of whom were volunteers and came from England, Australia, New Zealand and America. The team along with Paul worked in the hospital. Some members reviewed hospital systems and where possible made improvements. Paul completed surgical procedures in the small operating theatres, although sometimes, during the frequent power shutdowns, he ended up "suturing patients in the hallway, with the nurse holding a torch". Two-weeks later the team were reluctant to go home, as they realised there was so much more to be done to improve life in Rwanda.

Paul and another New Zealander, Trevor Walker, returned to Rwanda the following year to research how an effective contribution could be made. Subsequently 'Specialists Without Borders' (SWB), the Australian-based not-for-profit organisation was founded "to take the highest quality teaching into emerging countries". Garnering support from like-minded surgeons and other specialists was the next step, all of whom agreed to volunteer their time and pay their own expenses. Paul, with the commitment from 16 specialists from around the world, organised and facilitated a 10-day teaching seminar for doctors and nurses in Kigali, the capital city of Rwanda. Despite initial misgivings the seminar turned out to be very successful, suggesting that there was a great need for this type of culturally sensitive and up-to-date medical education.

Since then, 'Specialists Without Borders', has grown with almost 400 specialists, doctors and nurses now available to go and teach in developing countries. With independent financial support, SWB has evolved into a significant international teaching organisation that provides sustainable health education, more recently in Malawi and Zimbabwe www.specialistswithoutborders.org.

The experience in Africa with the significant social inequities, initiated Paul's second novel. 'Old Lovers Don't Die', which is a sequel to his first novel, with the characters reset in central Africa. While it again is a medical thriller, it incorporates the underlying social themes important to Paul, political manipulation, social inequality, racism, sexism and poverty. Paul said his thriller writing style, has been favourably compared to Jeffrey Archer and Bryce Courtenay by The Australian newspaper.

Back in Australia, between the yearly trips to Africa, Paul immersed himself in his growing private practice, lecturing to medical students, as well being a single dad to Jordan. He led a very busy life. On a regular visit to one of the private hospitals he was introduced to a new hospital manager, who captured Paul's heart and became the love of his life. Unfortunately, the relationship ended tragically when Donna frighteningly discovered she had uterine cancer. Paul went through the treatment ordeal with her, but sadly Donna died two years later.

Paul said his emotional adjustment was really difficult following Donna's death. Fortunately, his sister Gabrielle, who lived on the beach in Ōhope, over the hill from Whakatāne in New Zealand, was very supportive. She suggested that this was "the perfect setting for getting away from the stresses of life and surgery". Taking his sister's advice Paul bought a house on the beach in Ōhope. Along with his son Jordan, and their Golden Retriever Tia, they would visit the beach for four to six weeks each Christmas. His sister, he realised, was right. It was the perfect environment to de-stress and enjoy life again. This continued for several years, to the point where the neighbours looked forward to the return of the beautiful Golden Retriever each Christmas.

In 2015, while helping repair the roof of the shed, Paul fell off a ladder and fractured the heel bone in his foot. This type of injury can be quite severe and result in long-term complications, and in Paul's case, "the repair didn't go well and had to be re-done four times". The injury prevented Paul from being able to stand for the extended periods of time required in surgery, and he was unable to operate. It was a devasting blow. While he continued to be involved with Specialists

Without Borders, Paul wasn't ready or old enough to retire and so looked for another way to make a positive contribution. With time on his hands and with the encouragement of his female friends in Adelaide, who supplied stories to him, he wrote his first romance novel 'Love Cuts Deeper Than a Sharp Scalpel'. Paul said, "it was one of the most enjoyable to write".

In 2016, while recovering from further surgery to rectify his ankle at Ōhope Beach, he was offered a part-time lecturing position in the Department of Nursing at Te Whare Wānaga o Awanuiārangi, an indigenous tertiary institution in Whakatāne in the Eastern Bay of Plenty in New Zealand. Lecturing in medicine was Paul's other love, having lectured medical students at Flinders University medical school for 15 years. To fill in time he readily accepted a part-time lecturing position in anatomy, physiology, and clinical sciences. Paul had, in many ways, returned to his roots, to teach in a total immersion programme, in his home country. He immediately began to familiarise himself with the Māori health model encapsulating multiple dimensions (spiritual, mental, physical, environmental, and family health). This meant learning Te Reo and understanding the importance of Tikanga, especially as it applied to medicine. As Paul said, "learning Māori customs and traditions, allows doctors and nurses to be more culturally responsive, enabling them to better communicate with Māori patients and better understand the Māori view of health and healing". He said his recent immersion "has been an incredible learning journey, potentially identifying ways in which Māori health statistics may be improved in Aotearoa" (New Zealand). It was at this time that he completed his third medical thriller, which many have said is the best. All the characters from the previous novels have been reintroduced to Australia, where there is a storyline of a surgeon's wife, love, romance, drugs, the Mafia and Bikies.

In 2017, after his final ankle surgery, Paul was still unable to stand for the long periods required to operate. By this time, he had developed a growing appreciation of the local health issues in New Zealand, and the barriers to treatment. Concerned about the long waiting times to get to see a specialist and potentially have cancer treated, Paul opened a free Specialist Review Clinic in Kawerau. In this clinic Paul reviews urgent patients, to help prioritise their assessment and treatment in the public system. After a six-week trial period, the clinic was so successful the community established a charitable trust, called the 'Emergency Assessment Fund' to support the clinic to "help the financially disadvantaged with serious medical problems to get the help they need". The Specialist Review Clinic offers "assessment of acute medical problems for patients who would normally have to wait months before treatment in the overstretched public hospital system". Paul said, "the concept is supported in the region by the Eastern Bay of Plenty Primary Health Alliance, the government organisation that supports primary health care services through GP's".

The Specialist Review Clinic has proven to be a very successful initiative and very rewarding for those associated with it, with Paul also providing free surgical services for minor surgery. Paul is hoping that the concept will be accepted and promoted throughout New Zealand. Already an Australian medical publication has approached him to write an article about whether it could work in Australia. He said he thinks "it most definitely could"!

In 2019, Paul's son Jordan, who is also a doctor, came over from Adelaide, to assist him in the clinic. Paul says with a wry smile, the great fun that it was having a son tell him that he had left his sutures too long when they were cut!

Medicine, as Paul relates, has been a wonderful, shared interest for them both and continues to be a growing part of their relationship. Plans are currently underway to expand the service into a minor procedure centre, like a mini hospital, if there is sufficient support from the community and health organisations. For more information about the Emergency Assessment Fund and ways you can contribute, check out this website www.eafund.org.nz

Alongside his professional career, Paul takes responsibility for maintaining his own health and wellbeing. Now in his late 60's, he enjoys cycling and mountain biking most afternoons amongst the local farmlands. He also continues to pursue his creative interests. In 2018 he published a work of non-fiction, 'Fat off the right way' – a sustainable eating guide for weight loss and healthy living based on 15 years of experience running a surgical and weight loss clinic. All of Paul's books are available from online bookstores.

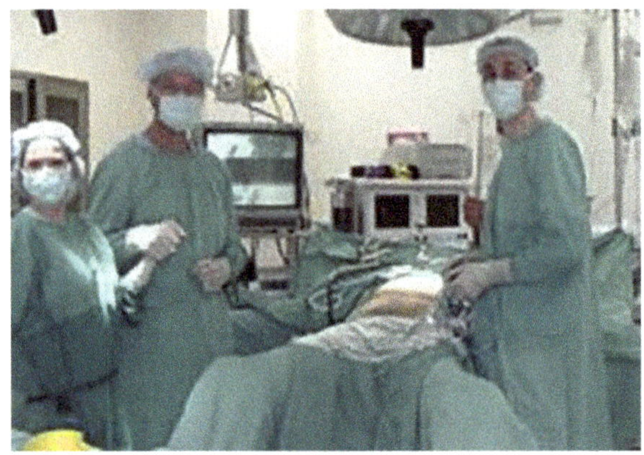

Laparoscopic surgery about to begin in theatre Dr Paul on the left with scrub nurse and assistant.

Paul Anderson and Prof Kate Drummond lecturing in Kigali Hospital, 2007

Tia

Paul's son Jordan at his graduation

Paul Anderson consulting

Paul cycling on Ōhope Beach

Paul's books are available from online bookstores

PAULINE AND JOHN BLAIKIE

Growing up in large families in the 1950's, Pauline and John came from similar backgrounds. Pauline's family were dairy farmers and John's family had a poultry farm. They met as teenagers at high school in Nelson. On leaving school the couple relocated to Wellington to continue their education, where the capital city offered more job opportunities. Pauline completed a secretarial course and John worked for the P and T (Post and Telegraph). In 1968, like so many young people looking for adventure, they took off on their big OE (Overseas Experience) to Australia. It was an exciting time. They spent the next two years travelling around Australia, doing lots of fun things along the way, and as there was plenty of work, they had no difficulty getting jobs to fund their trip.

When Pauline and John returned to New Zealand in 1970, they got married and once again settled in Wellington where they could get well-paid jobs and focus on their careers. John secured a job as a cable joiner with P and T (in later years this became Telecom), a large organisation that employed 26,000 people at the time. Pauline initially worked for Federated Farmers, and then in 1971 she got a job as a stenographer working for Norman Kirk, who in those days was the Leader of the Opposition in Parliament. Pauline really enjoyed her role working as part of a small team of five people led by Margaret Haywood, Norman Kirk's private secretary. Following the 1972 election, Norman Kirk, Leader of the Labour Party, became the Prime Minister and the Minister of Foreign Affairs. Accordingly, his administration team expanded, and Pauline moved into the larger typing pool. During his time as Prime Minister, Norman Kirk, who was hugely popular, became ill and died. Although he was succeeded by the then Minister of Finance, Bill Rowling, these were challenging times and, following the 1975 election, Rob Muldoon, the Leader of the National Party, became the Prime Minister. These changes naturally impacted on Pauline's role, with a change in leadership, she was once again working for the opposition (specifically, Mike Moore and Roger Douglas).

In 1976, Pauline and John started a family and with the arrival of their first son Peter, Pauline resigned from her job to take care of him. When their baby was just six months old, John was seconded to New Zealand Foreign Affairs Department to work in Apia, Western Samoa, where they were installing a new telephone exchange. John and Pauline saw this as a great opportunity and decided they would go to Samoa as a family for six months. They said, "it was a great experience for all of us and brings back fond memories of this stage in our lives". As they say, "the more experiences we have in life shapes who we are as we go along life's journey".

Back in New Zealand, the Blaikie family expanded with the arrival of their second son Matthew in 1979. Although John and Pauline enjoyed living in the city, now that they had a family they yearned for a different lifestyle, similar to the one they had experienced growing up themselves, so they began to look for a suitable rural property. Two years later they bought a mail delivery business in the Manawatū and moved onto a three-acre block which they immediately put to use growing produce. Within a few years, Pauline and John bought a 50-acre property in Rongotea and built a house on it. They managed 30 nurse cows on this property, that reared up to six calves each per year. They also raised free range chickens, producing free range eggs – a relatively new concept in the early 1990's. During this period, they also owned 150 acres at Mount Stewart where they raised bulls.

To supplement their income and to be able to achieve their goals, the couple managed the rural mail delivery run and bought a vat cleaning business, whereby they serviced the vats in fish and chip shops and supplied them with refined cooking oil. Whilst John carried out the day-to-day work in these two businesses, Pauline undertook full-time secretarial work for six years at Tui Milk Products in Longburn. They really enjoyed the lifestyle they had created for their family. They were able to draw on their previous farming experience when they were growing up, and more than anything Pauline and John were willing to put the effort in, work as a team, and give things a go. Inspired by what they had achieved over a 14-year period, it was time to look for a bigger rural property and do something different.

In 1995, Pauline and John found what they were looking for - a 300-acre property, in Rewa in the Manawatū. Surrounded by hill country, protected from the elements with a good climate, this rich river silt property was ideal to establish a sustainable certified organic farm. In a turmoil as they hadn't sold their other properties, the couple took the risk and went ahead and bought the Rewa property. They have never regretted it. They moved everything from their Rongotea property to Rewa – their family, personal possessions, a few cattle, 300 free-range chickens and their free-range egg production operation. They named their new property 'The Willows Organic Farm Ltd'. As soon as they could, they planted vegetables including peas, squash and carrots, grain to feed the chickens, and given the climate, developed a small orchard. They also applied for and were granted certification as an organic farm. Pauline and John were pioneers in this area. Their yield was better than the factory average and others were keen to learn from them. Wattie's bought their organically grown vegetables for processing and their squash was exported to Japan.

John and Pauline had complementary skills. They did their research, were prepared to learn through trial and error, and worked hard together as a team. John had good mechanical skills and not only fixed things; he designed and erected the purpose-built chicken sheds on their property from scratch. Within a short space of time, they increased their flock of hens from 300 to 8,000 – resulting in a significant growth in egg production and a very profitable commercial operation.

Pauline did all of the marketing herself. Initially she approached local supermarkets such as Write Price in Feilding. As the concept of organic free-range eggs was new, and they were more expensive to buy, prospective buyers were apprehensive about stocking them in the supermarket. To diminish their concerns Pauline offered the Manager of Write Price 15 dozen free-range organic eggs on consignment to see if their customers would be interested in them. That first consignment sold out very quickly and Write Price became one of the Blaikie's regular clients. As freight is so expensive, Pauline made the decision to restrict the distribution of their produce to the North Island which included New World supermarkets, Common-sense Organics, and any shops selling organic produce. Their free-range organic eggs became a very lucrative business and are sold under their own brand "Pasture Poultry", and "Bioland", which is an existing brand in the Auckland market.

Given there was so much interest in organic produce, the Blaikies took the initiative and set up a Central District Organic Growers Group to encourage like-minded people in the surrounding districts (Manawatū, Whanganui, Hawkes Bay and the Wairarapa) to come together for field days and learn with and from one another. Focused on continuous improvement, Pauline and John also took part in a government funded sustainable farming research trial led by Dr Alec Mackay, a senior scientist with the Agricultural Research Institute in association with Trevor Cook, a well-known veterinarian and farm advisor. Elements of this research was later televised on "Rural Delivery" and "Country Calendar" - television programmes showcasing New Zealand rural life.

Over the years, Pauline and John's children grew up and pursued their chosen careers in another district. The Blaikies remained on their farm and as their business went from strength to strength, they employed several local people to help them run it. Life was pretty good until disaster struck in 2004 when, without warning, a huge flood swept through The Willows Organic Farm. John said, "the silt from the Rangitīkei River was over fence height" and literally thousands (75%) of the Blaikies chickens drowned. This catastrophic flood, reportedly the largest in the Manawatū-Whanganui Region in recent times, was an indescribable knock-back for John and Pauline. Despite this massive hit, they surveyed the damage, prioritised what they needed to do, rolled their sleeves up and set to work. Pauline said, "communication in any scenario is number one" and she personally rang all of the people they supplied to explain the situation and reassured them they were still in business and would continue to service them. She also produced a newsletter which she included with every box of eggs that left their farm telling the customer their story and thanking them for their purchase. They cleaned out the chicken sheds and replaced the hens gradually to increase their egg production. The couple bounced back quickly, and as a result, they didn't lose their share of the market or any shelf space in the stores.

After the flood, John replaced the chicken sheds, redesigning and building them himself. The new sheds were built to a very high standard, "ensuring the eggs rolled away nice and clean". Subsequently Avian Vets rated The Willows Organic Farm as, "the best free-range set-up in New Zealand"! Pauline and John frequently hosted visitors from overseas who wanted to explore the set-up and they were always impressed. It helps that there are no predators such as foxes in New Zealand, and they were often told that they had "the best free-range operation in the world". John said the feedback they have received is "very satisfying and encourages you to keep going".

Whilst the farm is a seven-day-week operation, it's not been all work and no play for John and Pauline. The couple go for regular bike rides and have enjoyed several overseas holidays over the years. As John approached his 60th birthday, the family discussed how to celebrate this milestone. John has always been interested in mechanics and machinery, (a very useful skill to have when operating a farming business), and as a teenager enjoyed doing what teenage boys still love to do - racing cars! The decision was made to look at buying a race car, with the hope that John would have an off-farm interest to look forward to. A classic racing Mini was bought and presented to John at a surprise 60th birthday celebration! Since then, another classic race car, a BMW 6, has been purchased, and in that time much fun has been had at various race meetings around the country.

John and Pauline also enjoy time with their sons and four grandchildren who live approximately 100 kilometres away on the Kāpiti Coast. As they approached their 70's, mindful about the future, they began making plans for the next phase of their lives. In 2015, they bought a caravan and, although they didn't use it for a year, it was ready for when they needed it. Rather than move into a town, they decided to stay on their farm, keep their cattle and sheep, and look around for a suitable buyer for "Pasture Poultry". It had to be a buyer with the like-minded philosophy of the Blaikies and who were prepared to be "hands on" in the business to maintain their brand. In July 2018 they found the ideal buyer – people who were genuinely committed to organic egg production. "Pasture Poultry" was sold to two young families in the Hawkes Bay who had gone into business together. Keen to see the new owners do well, Pauline and John assisted in the move to Sentry Hill Farm in Hawkes Bay, transporting 8,000 chickens and chicken houses to their new home. This historic moment was captured on film for Country Calendar and was shown on TVNZ on demand later that year. To ensure a smooth handover, the Blaikies coached the two couples through the process, sharing everything they had learned over the years with them. Pauline and John are delighted that "Pasture Poultry" is in good hands and are thrilled that the new owners are doing really well making a success of their business.

Reflecting on their challenging experience, and their enormous ground-breaking success in organic agriculture, John makes the point, that growing up in the 1950's, their generation (the baby boomers), didn't have a lot of money, and this impacted on their thinking and how they spend their time and their money. He also feels strongly that every small business owner has to be "working in the business and they've got to be hands-on". He believes that if people are in business for the right reason and they enjoy it, "it will work". Both he and Pauline stress that "if you believe in your business, you are the best person to market it". Their philosophy, practice and resilience have certainly worked for them, and as they said they "have had a whole lot of fun along the way".

With more time on their hands, Pauline and John's son Matthew encouraged them to consider property investment in nearby Feilding, a town the Blaikies know well. The couple purchased their first rental property in 2016, sub-divided the section and built two affordable three bedroomed homes on it. They promptly purchased two more properties and repeated the process. Now, in addition to their farm in Rewa, which John and Pauline manage between them, they own and manage six three bedroomed rental properties and have really enjoyed the process. At the time of writing, Pauline, aged 71 and John, aged 72, lead very active lives. They love their rural lifestyle and are as active as they have ever been. Pauline's new nickname, given the "lockdown" under COVID-19, is "the squirrel" as she's been busy preserving and bottling the crops to ensure nothing is wasted. Meanwhile, John has been busy painting the roof and the walls of the house and the garage, and still works every day on the farm.

Thinking ahead, John and Pauline are conscious of ageing, but they have no plans to retire in the conventional sense. They enjoy the rural lifestyle and anticipate the need to downsize their acreage gradually. Realistically this may mean two moves for them, rather than a single move from the farm to a house in a small town - a decision they have observed others make and later regretted. Downsizing the acreage and associated stock and moving closer to their family and a town with its amenities comes first, and the move to a smaller home in a township comes later in life. This couple enjoy a challenge and take personal responsibility for the outcome. They appreciate it will take a couple of years to adjust to new routines with each move. At the same time, they want to ensure they can lead an active life in the years ahead of them, manage their property and their health and wellbeing and most importantly - don't get bored. Insightfully, Pauline and John recognise that retirement is not an event – it's a process that can take years.

The Willows Organic Farm Ltd.

John Blaikie with his racing cars

Pauline and John Blaikie on their farm

WIREMU WATI WARDLAW KORA

Ko Maungapōhatu te Maunga

Ko Tauranga te Awa

Ko Mata-Atua te Waka

Ko Tūhoe te iwi

Ko Tauanui te Marae

Ko Te Whakatāne te Hapū

Ko Wiremu Wati Wardlaw Kora taku ingoa

This is Wiremu's pepeha/genealogy. It describes who he is. Translated for you it means:

Maungapōhatu is Wiremu's Mountain

Tauranga is his River

Mata-Atua is his Canoe

Tūhoe is his Tribe

Tauanui is his Marae

Te Whakatāne is his sub-tribe.

Wiremu (Bill) was born in Waimana, in Te Urewera, one of NZ's national parks and homeland of the Tūhoe. He was given to another family, a whāngai, which is a customary Māori practice for children to be raised by other whānau (family) members. His whānga mother was 14 years old and after having Wiremu, 13 other children were to follow. His mother said, 'as soon as I got you son, I was able to have children'. As a youngster, Wiremu attended Waimana Primary School and then went on to attend Ōpōtiki College. He grew up in a predominantly Māori district, learnt tribal customs, tikanga, karakia and Te Reo (Māori language). Life was exceptionally hard for Wiremu growing up in his foster family. He recalls having to sleep out under blue gum trees, doing all the chores, bringing up the babies, washing the nappies and clothes, making the lunches, cleaning the house. He did these chores before and after school, and recalls being punished and severely beaten for virtually any minor misdemeanour. His worst experience was to cook the evening meal and then being told to get outside. Going without food was normal. As a young man he said he never really belonged to either his biological or his foster family.

When he left school Wiremu left home as soon as he could, first of all working as a farm labourer. He married when he was 16 years old. In today's world, this would be unheard of, but in 1966 in rural New Zealand, this wasn't unusual.

In the 1960's many young men, including Wiremu and his friends, were attracted to the armed services. Wiremu joined the New Zealand Army and off he went to Waiouru Military Camp in the central North Island to complete his initial basic training. He joined the Armoured Corps (the tankees) and loved not only his job, the training and his trade, but he really appreciated the camaraderie and shared experience with his peers. Earning good money, he was able to buy his first Jaguar car - his pride and joy. During this period New Zealand was involved in the highly controversial Vietnam war in accordance with the Australia New Zealand and United States security treaty (the ANZUS Pact). Several of his colleagues were posted to Vietnam and for most, it was their first trip overseas. When they returned home, they brought with them cars, tape decks, stereos, and all kinds of electrical equipment. To a young man it seemed like an exciting opportunity, so Wiremu volunteered to go and was eventually posted to a platoon with Victor 4 Company.

Prior to leaving for Vietnam, Wiremu and his platoon attended additional intensive training. They were also told that some of them would not return home from this war – but he and his colleagues didn't really believe anything would happen to them. Before he left for Vietnam, Wiremu, then aged 19, was blessed by the Tohunga, Taapapa, a Māori world priest, who told him that even though he would fight an enemy, that enemy was his host and would manaaki (look after) him and his friends. Reality struck when he found himself in the jungle. The Vietcong were the enemy (hoariri – angry friends), and they (the New Zealand troops) were on the Vietcong's home territory. When two of their friends were massacred, Wiremu and his mates wondered why they were there. He spent 15 months with Victor 4 Company in Vietnam (6 RAR/NZ (ANZAC) Battalion 1969-1970) and laughs when he recalls the bar at their base, aptly name the 'Never Inn' as they were rarely there.

Wiremu enjoyed the 12 years he spent with New Zealand Army, during which time he and his wife had two children – Jenny and Jason. While he was in Vietnam, he and a mate Andy Peters often talked about what they would do when they got home. One idea was to start a cadet unit for underprivileged young kids in Browns Bay, Auckland. Returning to New Zealand they formed the City of North Shore Cadet Unit. Andy, who was working as a prison officer at Paremoremo Prison, became the OC (Commanding Officer). Wiremu became the Administration Officer of the new unit. Young people from high schools and the streets of the North Shore joined the unit where they were taught the basics e.g., self-care, daily routines and cooperation. The aim was to steer them away from a life of crime, and potentially prepare them for a career in the Army, the Airforce or the Navy. Wiremu and Andy started the unit with few resources, but they had a mate who was the Quarter Master (QM) in the stores at Papakura Army Camp, which was only an hour's drive away. Andy and Wiremu needed clothes for these young people – "to instil a sense of belonging and a sense of pride, uniforms would be essential". These were duly obtained from the Papakura Q. Store, and the teenagers were taught how to wear them and how to care for them (e.g., washing, ironing, presentation skills etc.) along with other fundamental life skills. Over the next three years more than 60 young teenagers took part in the cadets. For many it was a life changing experience. Some of them did join the armed forces and they remain in contact with Wiremu to this day.

After serving 12 years with the military, Wiremu resigned and moved back to Whakatāne with his new wife Barbara. The couple loved music and decided to form a band. Barbara was a trained pianist through the London Guild of Music and learned to play the keyboards with great success. Wiremu was a guitarist/singer. They played a repertoire of rock, country, harmony, and dance music until they were comfortable playing as 'Bill and Barbara' in front of an audience. The couple set off from Whakatāne heading for the South Island. The duo 'Bill and Barbara' got their first gig at the Returned Services Association (RSA) Club in Picton, a small settlement in the Marlborough Region of New Zealand's South Island. The successful gig signalled the start of a new career for the couple. They subsequently contacted all of the RSA's in the South Island and offered to play to their members, many of whom were either in the military or were ex-servicemen and women. The income generated from their performances all over the South Island paid all of their bills, and they were able to buy a house in Timaru. They incorporated a recording studio, a disco and a karaoke business as well as looking after Ina, Wiremu's mother-in-law, "rest in peace Mum".

Whilst the couple enjoyed their music, Wiremu also enjoyed his voluntary work with young people, especially troubled youth. He knew first-hand how difficult teenage years can be for some young people. He also knew that he was fully versed in Māori Tikanga, customs and protocols, fluent in his native Te Reo (Māori language), was well connected in the Māori community and had the skills and life experience to help these young people turn their lives around. He facilitated Māori language courses at the Ashburton Learning Centre at night, as well as helping students to attain their driving licences. As a respected Māori elder (Kaumātua), Wiremu was often asked to facilitate family group conferences with various government agencies such as Work and Income, Social Welfare and the District Health Board in Timaru and their clients. In his spare time, he volunteered to help rangatahi (young children) and encouraged them to record their own songs onto compact discs in his recording studio. He also taught Te Reo in schools throughout the Timaru and Ashburton districts

After leaving Timaru, Wiremu and Barbara returned to Whakatāne. Wiremu was needed to help his marae, Tauanui. He was offered a position as a Student Support Adviser at Te Wānanga o Aotearoa in Whakatāne. Here he looked after many tauira (students). He quickly built rapport with the young people, assisting them in a myriad of ways. He helped them to apply for student loans and allowances, he provided pastoral care and advice on budgeting, and he assisted people with disabilities. Finance was particularly important as he didn't want the students to get into debt. Wiremu supported students with literacy and numeracy issues, helped them with their course studies and with the development of their curriculum vitaes. He also helped the students to gain employment when they had completed their studies. While employed at the Wānanga, following a visit from the Ministry of Education, Wiremu was awarded an honorary degree in recognition of his service, and was publicly recognised amongst his whānau as a Kaumātua (a respected tribal leader).

Wiremu also helps troubled youth, mainly young men, supporting them in and out of the court system. Gang members were a big focus for Wiremu. As a recognised Māori elder, he liaises with family members, Oranga Tamariki, (the Ministry for Children), the Police, the Family Court and the Department of Corrections and Te Kooti Rangatahi (Youth Court) at Wairaka Marae in Whakatāne. Over the decades Wiremu has touched so many lives across the spectrum of ages groups, and circumstances. It's his passion in life. He easily builds rapport with children, showers them with unconditional love and walks with them through times of crisis (e.g., court appearances and visits to residential facilities). Although he is a caring person with a big heart, he's also a straight talker. Drawing on his military background and experience, he takes no nonsense from anyone including gang members.

Late in 2019, Wiremu stepped back from his voluntary work to take care of his ailing wife. Barbara has since made a very good recovery and Wiremu is looking to see where else he can offer his services for the greater good of his community.

Wiremu, who is now in his 70's, has five adult children, (none of whom are in jail), ten mokopuna (grandchildren), and five mokopuna-tuarua (great grandchildren). They live throughout the globe. He also has two dogs (Rusty and Roxy), 48 hens, five roosters, 26 doves, quails, pūkeko, weka, tui and kereru adorning his section in Whakatāne. Wiremu still keeps in contact with his Victor 4 Company mates, and they regularly meet up at bi-annual reunions or at a mate's funeral. "May they rest in peace".

This photo of Wiremu (on the far left) was taken with the Queen Mother and her aides at a garden party in Windsor.

Wiremu Kora

RON AND LEONIE HAINES

Leonie was only 17 years old when she met Rod. He was in his early 20s, a brand-new lawyer, straight from university and she was appointed as his secretary at A. J. Park & Son, a law firm in Wellington. They worked well together and developed a great friendship, but over time they went their separate ways. Leonie moved to the South Island in order to see other parts of New Zealand. She later returned to Wellington, got married and had two children (Nicki and Steve). Rod joined a law practice in Kaitāia in the far north of New Zealand. Six years later he moved to the South Island where he and a chum from university set up a law practice (Carter:Haines) in Richmond, 13 kilometres south of Nelson, Rod's hometown.

Twelve years later, after Leonie's marriage had ended, she 'tracked Rod down, phoned him and told him I needed a friend and a lawyer'. Rod, who had always been fond of Leonie, immediately came to her aid. They renewed their friendship and became sweethearts. A year later Leonie (nicknamed Bunny) and her two children went to live with Rod in Nelson. In 1983 the couple got married and their family expanded to five with the arrival of their son Sam. They have been together ever since.

Rod had always wanted to be an engineer, but as he was born without arms, this wasn't a possible career option at that time. As a child he learned to write with his right foot and even won a handwriting competition while he was at school. While at University he learned to write again this time with an artificial arm with his left hand, so in his words he is 'ambidextrous'. He has since learned to two-toe-type on a computer. Despite many challenges, Rod became a very successful lawyer and Health Advocate, amongst other careers. He learned to drive and developed a passion for sailing.

Rod, who had always been interested in mechanical things, built a small outrigger canoe when he was at university. This was to be the first of the many boats Rod built and the beginning of a lifetime of adventure on the water. Rod introduced Leonie and the children to his love of sailing and the sea. The family often sailed in the estuary behind Nelson and the peaceful lagoons in the Abel Tasman National Park on the 'Dawn Treader' – a nine-metre trimaran Rod had built. Over the years that followed, they did a lot of sailing, but Leonie, who calls herself a 'picnic sailor' preferred cruising on the peaceful waterways and had to admit she didn't like being in rough water.

In 1998, after experiencing a four-day canal boat holiday on a traditional 47-foot narrowboat on the Llangollen Canal in the UK, Rod and Leonie were bitten by the canal boat bug. They loved the waterways, the scenery, and the tranquil lifestyle. On their return to New Zealand, Rod considered making alterations to the trimaran to re-create the cruising experience they had experienced in the UK. But, after weighing up the options, he chose instead to build another boat – this time a narrowboat of his own to cruise calmer inland waterways in New Zealand.

Rod designed 'Gentle' their houseboat to meet their specific needs. Together he and Leonie, who also became very adept at boat building, built it mainly using second grade plywood. Rod did the cutting (with his toes) and Leonie helped to assemble the parts. Leonie explained that 'he built everything below waist height, and I built everything above waist height'. The interior is like a caravan, the difference being that all the facilities are operated from a sitting position. The kitchen sink and stove are low down so that Rod can use his feet to light the gas stove, pump the water into the kettle, make the tea and serve it to Leonie before she gets out of bed. Inside the cabin Leonie made the soft furnishings and the houseboat is fully equipped for life on the water. It took about a year for the couple to build 'Gentle' and it truly was a team effort. The self-contained five metre craft is a caravan when strapped to the deck of a flat-bed trailer and an outboard powered boat when it's in the water. With Rod as the Deck Captain and Leonie as the Cabin Captain they launched their boat on Christmas Day 1999. Over the past two decades Rod and Leonie have towed their houseboat behind their family car all over the country, sailed it on numerous lakes and waterways and still have it to this day. The pleasure they have had from the houseboat over the years has been 'immeasurable'.

They had so much fun cruising with their family and friends that they encouraged others to 'have a go'. What concerned them was the size of a typical narrowboat on the canals in the UK, which can be difficult to handle in some situations, especially for two people. This discouraged some people and so Leonie and Rod came up with an idea. Why not design and build a shallow houseboat, less that 20-feet long, that had all the home comforts, could be handled by two people and was towable behind a family car? The couple completed two research trips to the UK before beginning the project. They formed a company, Gentle Cruising Co Ltd, in order to be taken seriously by the British Canal boating community.

Returning home, Rod set to work designing a couple of shallow houseboats, this time using aluminium, that could be folded down and shipped in a 20-foot container to the UK where they would be re-assembled. His dream was to sail the boats on British canals and exhibit them at the Narrow Boat Show in Crick. Rod and Leonie were both still working at the time, Rod as a health advocate with the Health and Disability Commission, and Leonie as a Resource Manager at Broadgreen Intermediate School in Nelson. This meant that most of the boat building was done in their spare time. Considering that they would need to transport the boats to the UK, and on arrival reassemble them in time for the boat show, Rod and Leonie had to take time off from their substantive jobs to meet the deadline.

Using Rod's innovative design for these vessels, they built two versatile 19-foot 6 inch fully self-contained floating caravans. These boats are half the length of a traditional narrowboat but have the same beam and height, are easier to manoeuvre on the water and are towable on the road. Essentially, their 'shallowboats', complete with New Zealand rimu timber interiors, have all the facilities and comforts of home, including a permanent double bed (a major feature), a single berth bed, a fully equipped galley and a bathing platform at the stern. With the support of family and friends, Rod and Leonie realised their dream. They packed and shipped the two 'shallowboats' to Portsmouth, England and reassembled them on arrival. It was an incredible accomplishment.

In England, Rod, Leonie and their son Sam (just 16), cruised the Grand Union Canal in their 'shallow boats', testing their manoeuvrability on the waterways and, with the help of their daughter Nicki, who was by then living in London, two nieces and some friends, exhibited 'Gentle Bunny' and 'Gentle Annie' at the Crick Boat Show in 2000. Unfortunately, it rained all weekend. As a result, fewer people came to this major boating event. After all their planning and hard work, it was disappointing. Nevertheless, the innovative design of 'Gentle Bunny' and 'Gentle Annie' caused 'quite a stir' amongst the traditional narrowboat community that did attend the show. After all Rod had designed these craft for maximum versatility. The crafts are usable both on the road and on the water – they are not reproductions of a traditional narrowboat.

After the Crick Show, Rod and Leonie had to return home. They left the 'Gentle Bunny' and the 'Gentle Annie' in the UK to be displayed at several different boat shows in their absence and had hoped to sell them. Despite great feedback from those who cruised the shallowboats in canals and positive reviews in 'Canal Boat and Inland Waterways' magazine, neither of the boats were sold. The boats were dismantled, packed back into a container, and shipped back to New Zealand.

Back home, Leonie and Rod returned to their professional roles. Gentle Cruising Company moved to Blenheim, in the heart of the Marlborough wine region in the northeast of the South Island. The area attracts tourists from all over the world and many appreciated the opportunity to cruise the waterways in the region.

Friends ran the day-to-day business for them, alongside their own Bed and Breakfast business, but when the latter was sold, 'Gentle Bunny' and 'Gentle Annie' went back home to Nelson. As time passed Rod and Leonie decided to sell both boats to private owners but have held on to 'Gentle', their pride and joy.

Rod retired from his job 12 years ago. During his long career he has been a lawyer, the Chair of a Hospital Board in Nelson, at one time he managed Nelson's psychiatric hospital, and was also a health advocate. He has been a referee at the Disputes Tribunal and was the first appointed Wellington Manager of the Privacy Commission when it was set up in New Zealand. Leonie retired from her position as Principal's PA at Garin College in Nelson, nine years ago. Clearly, they have always encouraged one another, and their children, to follow their passion, dream big dreams, be innovative, have a go, learn and apply new skills. Importantly they have always worked as a team.

In retirement, the couple relocated to Levin in the Horowhenua where they lived for 18 months. About six years ago they moved to Foxton Beach in the Manawatū-Whanganui region of New Zealand. Here they are slowly renovating their home and now enjoy a relaxed lifestyle close to the banks of the Manawatū River where they can cruise on their boat. The couple have forged friendships within this community and are members of the local Rebus Club (formerly a Probus Club.) Family has always been a priority for Leonie and Rod. Two of their three adult children live in New Zealand, and one lives in London. They have been blessed with four grandchildren. Since retiring Rod has written 'Armless Not Brainless' – it's an inspirational book about his life and the couple's cruising experience on 'Gentle'.

Both he and Leonie have often been approached to speak to community groups and organisations about their experiences, which they used to thoroughly enjoy. Several articles about their lives and experiences have been published in local and international boating and lifestyle magazines. With lots of encouragement from family and friends the couple were contemplating writing a second book about their lives, but Rod was recently diagnosed with Parkinsons, which is slowing them both down a bit. However, the idea is still on the drawing board.

In December 2020, at a nationally televised event celebrating the achievements and successes of New Zealanders living with disability, Rod's triumph of ability over disability and his lifetime dedication to the sector was formally acknowledged when he was inducted into the Attitude Lion Foundation Hall of Fame. In her citation at the event the Honourable Ruth Dyson said, "Rod has always exceeded expectations. His ingenuity and ability to navigate any challenge has provided an example for others and his generosity has benefitted New Zealanders of all abilities. It is a great honour to induct you, Rod, into the Attitude Hall of Fame". It was a moving tribute for an incredibly deserving recipient, and a proud moment for the whole family who attended the event.

Rod's book is available from online bookstores. They also have hard copies available if you would like to email them at randlhaines@gmail.com

Rod and Leonie onboard Gentle

Parked up at home.

Rod cutting aluminium with plasma cutter

Leonie having her turn

Rod with Gentle Bunny

Gentle Bunny on English canal (Sam driving)

Gentle Annie on Opawa River, Blenheim with the local Mayor

Rod's book

Rod, Leonie, and their family at the NZ Attitude Awards 2020

BOB AND IRENE HOSKINS

As teenagers, Bob and Irene went to Christchurch West High School in the South Island. They met when they both took part in their high school musical 'Pirates of Penzance' and have been together ever since. On leaving school Irene, who wanted to be a teacher, went to Christchurch Teachers Training College. Bob, who from the age of ten had planted trees in the wetland at Waimakiriri River in Canterbury on Arbour Day each year, was interested in the sciences. Initially he aspired to be a doctor, but while studying for a Bachelor of Science at the University of Canterbury, he became captivated with zoology and geology. He later graduated with a Bachelor of Science with honours in Zoology, and a Master of Science in Geology. The young couple both enjoyed their studies and encouraged each other to follow their passion. In 1966, when they turned 21 years of age Irene and Bob got married.   Irene began her teaching career at Christchurch schools (Ilam and Aorangi), and Bob who was interested in micropalaeontology (the branch of palaeontology that studies micro fossils), worked part-time operating a rock crusher for material used in making Terazzo whilst studying.

After graduating with his Master's degree, the couple moved to the Hutt Valley where Irene secured a teaching role at Naenae School in the Hutt Valley. Bob secured a role in the New Zealand Geological Survey Division of the Department of Scientific and Industrial Research (DSIR).   In his DSIR consultancy role, Bob dated rocks for the Oil Industry and for geologists mapping the country. He loved this role and found the work in petroleum, a multimillion-dollar industry, totally consuming. Reflecting back on these days, he said he "loved this job so much" he "would have done it for nothing". During this period, he undertook field trips all over New Zealand and enjoyed tramping with his friends in the Tararua Ranges, one of several mountain ranges in the North Island of New Zealand. Bob, who was very successful in his role at the DSIR, was given the opportunity to undertake a PhD in his field of specialisation with the support of a National Research Advisory Council scholarship. In the early 1970s, scientific staff at the DSIR were encouraged to undertake further study and develop their expertise, so Bob jumped at the opportunity. By this time the couple had two children (a daughter aged four and a son aged two) and, after talking it over with Irene, the family moved to the United Kingdom while Bob undertook his doctoral fellowship in Bristol and Exeter. Four years later, with his research thesis on 'New Zealand Middle Miocene Foraminifera: The Waiauan Stage' completed, Bob graduated with his doctorate in Geology.

In 1978, the family moved back to New Zealand. Irene obtained a teaching role with Rātā Street School in Lower Hutt, where she taught for the next 16 years, and Bob went back to his job at the DSIR. Life was good for the next decade or so. Irene and Bob loved their work and daily life in the Hutt Valley, and while their children were growing up the couple bought a beach house for the family in Foxton. In Bob's role he had the opportunity to work overseas, attend conferences and he hosted internationally recognised industry experts in New Zealand. He worked 16-hour days with unrestricted use of machinery, visited oil rigs and undertook fieldwork, it was in his words "a brilliant job". Regrettably, in 1992 everything changed. The DSIR was restructured into a number of 'user pays' Crown Institutes and many of the scientists, including Bob, were made redundant. Although Bob was only 45 years old at the time, large numbers of staff, who were also in niche jobs in New Zealand, were made redundant, so there were limited employment opportunities. In the first six months after leaving the DSIR, Bob said he applied for more than 400 jobs without success. It was very disheartening as he was considered to be 'overqualified' for most of the jobs that were available.

Bob considered his transferrable skills which included his expertise with technology, DIY skills, people skills, research skills, and his ability to source and interpret and write technical information so he contacted the workplaces that required these skills. He omitted his post-graduate qualifications from his curriculum vitae to maximise his chances of getting interviews. He obtained work in the Patent Office Library where he helped people apply for patents and researched applications for patents. During this period, Irene was teaching, the children had grown up and left home to follow their own career paths, and Bob considered his longer-term career prospects. An avid reader, in mid-life he made the decision to re-train as a librarian and while he worked his day job, he completed his training by distance education over a two-year period.

In 1995, when Bob applied for a sole charge librarian's role in Foxton and was duly appointed to the job, he and Irene sold their house in Lower Hutt and moved into their beach house in Foxton. They had always enjoyed spending time at their beach house, were familiar with the community, and appreciated the foreshore and the Manawatū Estuary which was recognised by the Ramsar Convention as being one of the few wetlands of international significance. In this location they were also close to the Tararuas so Bob could continue to pursue his tramping and geological activities. Irene secured a teaching role at Foxton Beach School and so began a new chapter in Bob and Irene's lives. As Bob was a keen hiker, he volunteered to help maintain walking tracks in the Tararuas until the Department of Conservation no longer required this form of support. This project included voluntary work developing the Te Araroa national trail in New Zealand, (Kaitāia to Bluff), and in particular the Mangahao-Makahika Track. This is no mean feat when you consider Bob needed to hike the 900-metre ascent carrying a chainsaw and a pick before continuing his days' work on the trail.

Both Irene and Bob enjoy the outdoors and are passionate about the environment. They often visited wetlands when they went on holiday and had planned to grow bamboo and make paper when they retired, but this plan never happened. Living and working in Foxton, they were appalled when they saw the state of the Manawatū Riverloop at Foxton, known as "The Loop".

They observed the results of the piecemeal flood relief work that had been undertaken by the drainage boards and the Government on the Manawatū river and realised that regrettably the original project hadn't been successful. The short-term solutions had caused significant long-term issues to the environment. Everything in The Loop was overgrown. The plant and animal life and the environment were increasingly affected. Steps needed to be taken to rectify the situation, so Bob raised the issue with the Regional Council, offered free geological advice and made lots of submissions, but to no avail.

In 2005 Bob joined the 'Save Our River Trust' – SORT, which was established to "promote the restoration and conservation of the Foxton Loop Piriharakeke for the benefit of the community".

Members of this charitable trust formed four teams who worked to improve the environment of The Loop. Initially Bob led the walkway team that built a walkway called Piriharakeke Walkway that went through the pine forest by the Manawatū Riverloop at Foxton. When he retired in 2007, he became more involved in the Save Our River Trust. Given his passion and expertise, Bob took on a planning and coordinating role and led three other teams: the planting team, the weed removal team, and the gardens team. When Irene retired from her teaching role after 16 years at Foxton Beach School, she also took on a more active role with the Trust.

The mission for the Save Our River Trust is more than a beautification project; it is a restoration project. Over the past 15 years members of this community have put in tens of thousands of hours on a voluntary basis to literally tackle the problem to "save our river". They have undertaken all the physical work themselves. Over a fifteen-year period, they removed hundreds of invasive willow trees that were strangling the eco-system. They also removed the rubbish and noxious weeds that were smothering the native plants, clogging the river, destroying the natural habitat for the birds and the fish, and spoiling the native flora and fauna. Members of the group continue to use their own tools (chainsaws, mowers, spades, strimmers, trailers etc.). They buy weed killer out of their own pockets and transport the rubbish they collect in their own vehicles to the local tip, often paying the tip fees themselves. It is evident that this equipment needs to be replaced over time, and they need industrial rather than general gardening equipment. They also needed to purchase native plants to create a new environment where whitebait, plant and birdlife could thrive. Whilst Bob and Irene grew some of the plants themselves in their garden, they recognised they would need more established plants in considerably larger numbers than they could grow themselves. Some plants have been provided by the Regional Council.

The Trust applied for funds from various sources, submitted plans for walkways with detailed cost analysis for the appropriate tools and native plants, submitted applications for resource consents and sought support from both the Horowhenua District Council and Horizons Regional Council. It's unfortunate and insulting, but often true, that retired volunteers are not taken seriously by the paid workforce, regardless of the extent of their qualifications and expertise. Sadly, this was the case for Doctor Bob and the River Trust who finally engaged and funded a consultant to obtain resource consents on their behalf – consents that they had already completed themselves.

Despite the frustrations, the Trust's persistence, environmental research, personal investment, hard work, numerous meetings and good documentation produced results. In due course, Horizons Regional Council became hugely supportive of the work the Trust has done and continues to undertake. Several grants were subsequently obtained enabling the Trust to pay some of the fees for the resource consents and fund the operation of equipment and planting of giant native flax plants.

The Regional Council acknowledges the vision, organisation, dedication, and the physical work members of the Trust have undertaken on a voluntary basis to proactively preserve and protect the natural environment. The eco-system in the Manawatū River is slowly being restored, the Foxton Loop Walk has been transformed, and the wildlife is returning. It is a massive achievement. This project is a credit to the community – a natural habitat people can enjoy for generations to come.

To this day Bob and Irene, who are now in their 70's, still collect rubbish from the foreshore and the estuary on a voluntary basis, and they transport it and pay the dumping fee themselves, rather than see the work of the Trust unravel.

Irene also provides morning tea for each of the working teams each week from the family's personal budget. This couple changed their plans for retirement to invest in something bigger than themselves for their community and the visitors who are drawn to the Horowhenua each year.

Although the past 15 years have had their ups and down, overall, their work with the Trust has been a labour of love and very rewarding. Whilst the Trust is still as active as ever (it is currently embarking on a feasibility study for a wetland that will deal with stormwater from Kings Canal in Foxton), Bob acknowledges that none of the Trust members are getting any younger. His focus is on succession, explaining that it will take ongoing work to maintain a functional eco-system such as this for future generations. It takes considerable energy to operate power tools and undertake physical labour for several hours a day. So, "who", Bob asks, "will pick up the reins? Will a younger generation of volunteers maintain and continue the Trust's work to develop and protect this environment, or will the District and/or Regional Council step in"?

Bob and Irene in their home

What happened to our river at Foxton?

The original path of the Manawatu River was unintentionally redirected to bypass Foxton in 1942 when the Government Works Department were clearing a new route to construct a flood-protection weir. During construction an actual flood occurred and forced its way through the partly completed Whirokino Cut - thus nullifying the work to create the weir and diverting the main route of the River.

In 1949 The Minister of Works admitted responsibility for 'righting the wrongs' and in 1953 a Commission of Inquiry acknowledged that central government had made a mistake and need to address this - but almost 70 years later still no restorative action has been taken.

Over the years the shut-off of river flow to the top end of the loop has resulted in complete blockage causing so much degradation that the waterway is deemed toxic to all forms of life.

The 'Save Our River Trust' explains what happened to the river at Foxton in their brochure 'The Manawatū River Loop at Foxton'

Using their own tools on the restoration project

Planting the giant native flax plants

Rubbish collected in a couple of hours at the foreshore.

Bob, enjoying a well-earned rest in a wheelbarrow.

MAURICE AND SANDRA POWELL

Maurice was born in Mataura, a papermill town in the Southland region of the South Island near Gore. He was the third of six children and the oldest boy in the family. When the family moved to Invercargill, Maurice and his siblings went to school. His father was an engineer on a fishing boat and the nature of his work took him away from home for up to six-weeks at a time catching crayfish in Fiordland. In those days, the fishing catch was flown to Invercargill in seaplanes with Monk Airlines. Maurice's Dad used to send a telegram asking Maurice to meet him when he came home to Invercargill with the fish. As Maurice was the oldest boy he was sometimes treated to a ride in the plane to Fiordland and back with a load of crayfish which was "great fun"!

On leaving school, Maurice secured an apprenticeship at J.J. Nivens and four-years later became trade qualified as a Fitter Turner. He loved fiddling with cars, especially his father's car, and bought a 1937 Velocette motorbike which was his pride and joy.

As a youngster a group of his friends suggested they live in Auckland in the North Island, 1,640 kilometres away. It seemed like a good idea, so the lads packed up their belongings, jumped on their motorbikes and biked to Picton to catch the ferry to Wellington and then biked the remainder of the trip to Auckland. When they arrived, they rented a flat with seven beds, to accommodate all of them, above Wades' shoe shop in

Karangahape Road.   Maurice recalls this being a great adventure for everyone as it was the first time any of the youngsters had been away from home. He was lucky to get an engineering job at a small friendly tool and die making business and during the two years he worked there he learned a lot about this industry. Although it was fun, it was expensive to live in Auckland, so Maurice and a mate rode their motorbikes to Christchurch where they intended to live for a while. The plan changed when the lads decided to tackle an overseas adventure, their first stop being Sydney, Australia where a few of their kiwi friends lived. They flatted with their friends in Glebe and got jobs as soon as they could. Maurice worked for an engineering firm in Glebe for a while and then he and his three kiwi friends began to explore Australia together.

Maurice and his friends left Sydney heading north up the eastern coast of Queensland to Mackay; a city nicknamed the sugar cane capital of Australia, as more than a third of Australia's sugar is produced in this region. In Mackay Maurice took a job installing fire sprinklers in the roof with Wormald Brothers, where he was highly regarded. Within a short space of time, he was asked if he would complete a job at Swan Brewery in Darwin in the Northern Territory. He saw the job offer as a great opportunity to see more of Australia and the pay was good, but by this time he'd met Sandra, who lived in Mackay, and they had become close friends. As the contract was only for three months Maurice took the job and moved to Darwin in 1967. Shortly after, Sandra left her home and her job and travelled nearly 3,000 kilometres to join him.

Darwin, situated on the Timor Sea, is both the capital city and the largest city in the sparsely populated Northern Territory. In those days, Darwin was a prosperous frontier-like city. Ninety percent of the 47,000 strong population worked for the Government and it had an Army, Airforce, and a Naval base. Although the city was quite isolated in the Northern Territory, Maurice and Sandra quickly realised there were lots of opportunities and they could build a good life together in this location. The couple got married in April 1969 and began to plan their future together.

For the next seven years they worked incredibly hard to realise their dream of living in the Australian outback – a lifestyle they relished. At one time Sandra was working three jobs, they developed a savings plan and bought two freehold properties, one of which was a five-acre block located on Darwin's main water source.

By Christmas 1974, everything was going according to plan when disaster struck on Christmas Eve. Cyclone Tracy, a tropical cyclone with wind gusts recorded at up to 217 kilometres an hour before the instruments failed, swept through the city over a two-day period leaving devastation in its wake.

Seventy-one people were killed and there were hundreds of casualties. The cyclone totally destroyed 70% of Darwin's buildings, and 80% of its houses causing millions of dollars' worth of damage. Approximately 30,000 people, more than half the original population, became homeless and sought shelter in makeshift emergency centres, but there was basic sanitation with limited access to water and electricity. The threat of disease in the tropical climate was high. As the official communication channels were no longer operational, a network of amateur radio connections was established. Many people were traumatised by the experience, a state of emergency was declared, and a major disaster relief operation ensued pulling on official resources supported by volunteers from all over Australia.

More than 35,000 people were evacuated. Maurice and Sandra were amongst those who chose to remain in Darwin to help with the clean-up, but they had nowhere to live and were distraught – they had lost everything, including their dream. Distressed they packed up their car with the few belongings they had left, including their cat, and drove 1,600 kilometres to Mount Isa where many of the evacuees from Darwin had sought refugee status and support. In the aftermath of Cyclone Tracy, 'Mount Isa Mines' transported hundreds of people and vehicles 900 kilometres further south to Townsville in the mine's railway wagons. Luckily, Maurice and Sandra were amongst the last of the refugees to leave Mount Isa for Townsville. On this journey they recall the train stopped frequently so that the passengers could get off and stretch their legs, while volunteers from the various townships along the route kindly provided them with water and rations. Disembarking the railway wagon in Townsville, Maurice drove another 400 kilometres to Mackay so they could be reunited with family. The young couple had suffered huge personal and financial loss and their dream was shattered.

Traumatised by the experience they considered how they

would rebuild their lives and made the decision to move to New Zealand to be close to Maurice's family. Maurice and Sandra said it took years for them to recover, but they "met the right people who supported them when they needed it most". They both secured jobs in New Zealand and Maurice's new boss helped them to get a loan to buy a house in the Hutt Valley. Sandra, who had always loved the outdoors developed a keen interest in gardening. Maurice, who maintained his interest in motorcycles, repaired motorbikes as a hobby. He bought a Norton Commando motorbike, joined the Norton Owners Club and explored many of New Zealand's roads with fellow members. Four years after leaving Australia, the couple started a family. Whilst raising their children, Glenys and Anthony, Sandra worked at the Inland Revenue to supplement the family's income.

The years passed and the children grew up and left home. Glenys got married and she and her husband had a family of their own. Maurice and Sandra enjoyed their jobs and continued to work. Both Maurice and Sandra had always been active. They appreciate the outdoors and on workdays Maurice loved his lunchtime aerobics classes. His first heart attack came as a complete surprise during one of these classes. He doesn't recall the incident, but he does remember waking up in the ambulance on the way to the hospital. Once diagnosed, a stent was inserted, and his recovery began. Maurice said his level of fitness had carried him through the shock of the attack and so he resumed his lunchtime aerobics class. All went well until he experienced a second heart attack following a motorcycling trip around the South Island. This time he recognised the symptoms and immediately sought medical help. To ensure he maintains his level of fitness he follows a regular exercise programme to this day.

When Maurice retired in 2008, aged 65, he and Sandra bought a section in Raumati. As a retiree, Maurice worked with a local builder for 20 months to build their new home to their own specifications. During this period, Sandra continued to work at the Inland Revenue Processing Centre in Upper Hutt. As they are keen cyclists, they and their friends, formed a cycling club and regularly get together to cycle around the district. Throughout their married life the couple had always planned to return to Australia and tour the outback. In late 2009, after the house building project had been completed, Maurice flew to Australia and purchased a four-wheel drive Land Cruiser. When he returned home, mission accomplished, Sandra resigned from her job and they packed up their belongings, put them into storage and rented their house out. Within four weeks they were back in Queensland Australia, to "work, travel and play" as grey nomads.

As freedom campers Maurice and Sandra spent five years in Australia catching up with family and friends. During this time, they revisited places they had been to when they first met and explored national parks and the outback. To get casual work they drafted an advertisement offering to do all kinds of handyman, gardening, farming, and domestic work on the stations in the outback. They posted their ad in the 'Positions Wanted' column of the monthly farmers magazine called 'Outback'.

Fewer younger people wanted to live and work in the outback, so help was scarce. Consequently, Sandra and Maurice always got a good response to their adverts and obtained work in and around the Great Dividing Range. They have an affinity with animals, loved the outdoors and often worked for several weeks at a time at any one station, which suited their lifestyle.

In 2010 and early 2011, Australia experienced what is known as the 'Big Wet'. Severe tropical rains hit the country. Essentially there was 50% more rainfall than normal causing a series of flooding events in Queensland, the Northern Territory and Victoria. The enormity of the damage was horrendous - roads, homes, farms and stock were washed away. It was another major disaster for people living in rural and urban communities. In particular, the people living in remote areas were isolated and needed all the help they could get. Homes and livelihoods were lost, people were displaced, and stock was lost. Maurice and Sandra recognised the impact this would have on the community and reached out with offers to help in whatever way they could. As they were prepared to travel over rough terrain to isolated areas in the outback, their services were in high demand. Reflecting on their experience they said they "did all kinds of work" and "met all sorts of characters". What's more they developed strong friendships with many of their clients, many of whom they keep in touch with to this day.

In 2014, the couple came back to their home in Raumati, New Zealand. Maurice likes carpentry work and as a handyman was quite good at it, so he joined a woodworking group and now likes to make and repair furniture. Sandra has always enjoyed gardening and quickly got to work on their section. She also likes to sew – either making clothes or household items from scratch (e.g., curtains), or making alterations to existing items, smartening them up and giving them a new lease of life. Four years ago, the couple decided to learn to play a musical instrument. Sandra's choice was the ukulele. Maurice bought himself three harmonica books and a mouth organ and taught himself how to play it. He also plays several percussion instruments. The couple joined 'Kāpiti Strummers' - a local ukulele group that meets twice a week to practice. This group also performs gigs for the local community.

In their 70's, outdoor exercise is still very important to the Powell's. When they came back home, they took up cycling again with their friends in the cycling club. By this time the membership of the group had grown from 10 to 60 members. In the past 12 months they have invested in e.bikes using the pedal assist function when required, reducing the pressure on the knees and shoulders when cycling long distances. Maurice cycles the local tracks four times a week. Sandra cycles twice a week and aqua jogs once or twice a week at the local swimming pool.

Catching up with friends, they shared their story about their years in Australia, and their gardening/caretaking/handyman work and their love of animals. Before long, friends were asking them to house-sit for them and take care of their pets when they went on holiday. During these 'homestays' Maurice does any handyman chores that need doing, while Sandra tidies up the gardens. They both take care of animals which to date have included chickens, dogs, cats, doves, goats, sheep and cows.

Sandra and Maurice cherish their family and love to spend time with their two grandchildren who live in Auckland. Friends are also important, whether they are local or thousands of kilometres away in the outback of Australia. Sandra says, "it's easy to get in touch using the latest technology, but you can't beat writing and receiving an old-fashioned letter – it makes someone's day to know you are thinking about them".

Maurice with his Velocette motorbike

Maurice and Sandra as newly-weds.

https://ntl.nt.gov.au/story/cyclone-tracy

http://www.abc.net.au/news/2014-12-24/darwin-remembers-cyclone-tracy-40-years-on/5986770

Maurice with his Norton and friends from the motorcycling club

ACTIVE semi retired couple. Kiwi handyman
/builder/painter/engineer
/gardening/caretaking.
Own c/van. **0428 481 835**

The advertisement Maurice and Sandra posted in 'Outback'.

Maurice and Sandra

Maurice and Sandra with their daughter, son-in-law,
and their grandchildren

BARBARA McGOWAN

Barbara was the first British baby born in Berlin, Germany after the war. Her father, a Captain Quartermaster in the British Army, was assigned rehabilitation duties for prisoners of war in Berlin. Her mother, who was born in Cape Town, South Africa, was a nurse. Barbara described her parents as being treated as if they were part of the British aristocracy, but she said that in reality they were "down to earth people". Barbara has three siblings, an older brother named Arthur who was born in London on D-Day within the sound of Bow Bells, a younger brother Cecil, born in Gottingen, and a younger sister Dorothy, who was born in Hanover.

The family travelled a lot after the war dependent on her father's military postings which included several years in Malaysia and Singapore. In Singapore Barbara's mother worked as a nurse at Singapore General Hospital and the children attended school. Barbara remembers being the only English girl at Crescent Girls School; the Headmistress, Miss Norris, was the only other European in this multi-racial school that offered a liberal education, valued diversity and was very inclusive. Barbara recalls English was the primary language used, but she also learned to speak Malay and Chinese dialects as well as Hindi and Pigeon English. Although Barbara was not Singaporean, as a youngster she was also actively encouraged to take part in preliminary swimming trials leading up to the 1964 Olympics.

In 1958, when Barbara's father was demobbed from the British Army, he got a job as an Army Press Reporter for a further two years. Her parents applied to migrate to New Zealand (NZ), where her dad applied to the NZ Army and was given the position of payroll officer. The family packed up their belongings and drove their car onto the 'Johan van Oldenbarnavelt' – the Dutch immigrant ship that took them, along with their granny to New Zealand.

Barbara remembers that when her father was ever asked if he had any hand luggage, he would point at his four children and say yes, A B C and D, who all wore labels with their first initial and 'E' for Edmonds, which was their surname.

The ship finally docked in Wellington Harbour at the end of 1960 but unfortunately, the festive season was in progress. In those days few people worked over the Christmas/New Year period and most businesses literally closed down for the summer holiday period (most of January); in this culture it was a time when families traditionally took their vacations. With few staff working on the wharf and in Customs, unfortunately the family could not access their belongings or their car, which could not be released until it had been fumigated in accordance with New Zealand's biosecurity regulations. Heavily dressed, as the temperature on arrival was a lot cooler than they were accustomed to in Singapore, the family sought accommodation, but given the season, little was available to them. The difference between the bustling city of Singapore and Wellington city seemed immense.

In Wellington, the family that had always travelled together, had to be separated. Barbara's father and her two brothers lodged together on The Terrace, while her mother and grandmother lodged together in Wellington. Barbara and her sister were found a room at the Kings Cross Hotel in the Hutt Valley 23 kilometres away from their family in Wellington city. Barbara, then in her early teens, and her sister were living in a public house in the days when the 'six o' clock swill' – a 'temporary' wartime referendum that was still in place in the 1960's, in which patrons drank their fill before the 6pm closing time. Back then The Kings Cross Hotel was a favourite watering hole and Barbara recalls being petrified when patrons poured into the hotel and left practically inebriated at six o'clock. Fortunately, the landlady of the hotel kept an eye on them while they were in her care.

Barbara said she and her sister looked forward to the train ride into Wellington to meet their father. Fortunately, within a few weeks the family finally managed to rent a six bedroomed house in Kelburn, one of the Wellington suburbs. When the school year began in February, Barbara and her sister were both registered to attend Wellington Girls College. Walking to school one day the girls were astonished to see the family's car being driven through the streets of Wellington. They later learned the car was on its way to be fumigated before the family were allowed to drive it on the same streets!

Barbara's high school experience in New Zealand was not a happy one. From Barbara's perspective, the school curriculum was traditionally conservative, conformist and conventional rather than progressive, and the culture seemed less inclusive.

It was a complete contrast to what she had experience in Singapore. Although Barbara was proficient in maths and languages, she had enrolled in a homecraft course as she wanted to be a dietician. She quickly learned that the education system was unlike what she had been accustomed to in Singapore. Having been brought up in war-torn countries, she and her siblings had all learned to be fully independent. In addition to being able to speak several languages they could cook and sew and were encouraged to express their opinions. Barbara discovered this was not necessarily the 'norm' when exposed to a new and different culture, with a discrete curriculum.

Students in the homecraft stream were not considered to be very bright, regardless of their talent, and she found the classes uninspiring. Already a gifted dressmaker, when given the opportunity to select a garment to make, Barbara chose to make a gold lame fully lined suit, which was an unusual outfit for a young person in this environment. Although a challenging project for a teenager, she completed the assignment, and wore the outfit, which she still has to this day, but she also remembers how scornful her teacher and peers were about it. This wasn't an isolated incident. Ostracized by their fellow students, she and her Indian friend Nirmala were labelled "curry munchers". Clearly this is unacceptable behaviour today, but was tolerated in the 1960's. In retaliation Barbara got into a lot of trouble and one fateful day a girl in her class cut off one of Barbara's braids. Incensed, Barbara threw an apple at the culprit giving her a black eye, and as a result Barbara was suspended. Barbara was mortified, not only because she was suspended, but also her long beautiful hair which had been her father's pride and joy had been cut.

It's no surprise Barbara left school as soon as she could. She took a job at J.J. Ilotts, an advertising agency where she had already been working on a part-time basis while she was a student and full time during the holidays. Here she had the opportunity to put her mathematical skills to work. When the Assistant Accountant resigned to go overseas, Barbara was offered the role, as the managers appreciated that she was good with figures. This was a turning point in her life and her career. Barbara worked as the Assistant Accountant for J.J. Ilotts for four years and gained further business and accounting experience in roles with Cubit Wells, J.J. Nivens, Price Waterhouse, Hunt Duthie & Co, and McKissick and Andrews. Tay Wilson, one of the partners with McKissick and Andrews later started his own company named 'Tay Wilson & Co., Accountants'. Tay recognised Barbara's ability and potential, employed her, became her mentor and encouraged her to get a formal qualification in her field.

While working for Tay Wilson & Co she secured a supervisory role and following the 1976 Olympics she helped Tay establish rowing within New Zealand colleges. All this time Barbara was working full-time as a solo Mum with two children Carol and Debbie. After her marriage to Donald McGowan, she had two more children – a daughter, Barbara Jnr, and a son named Jimmy. Tay Wilson became Jimmy's godfather. As the children were born within 15 months of one another Barbara took three months off work to care for them before returning to work full-time. Although she was extremely busy, with her parents and Tay's support she attended night school, gained her qualification, and became a member of the Chartered Institute of Secretary's and Administration. It was a huge achievement and tremendously beneficial to her long-term career.

Barbara bought a home in Brooklyn, a suburb in Wellington where she raised her family. In the years that followed, the children grew up and left home. Sadly, Barbara's father passed away in 1974, and her ageing mother became wheelchair bound in 1982.

Barbara and her sister Dorothy, who lived in Ōtaki, both wanted to care for their mother who was a double amputee and had serious medical conditions. Intending to live closer to one another, they looked for a suitable property in the Horowhenua / Ōtaki area and found the ideal house in Manakau, 81 kilometres north of Wellington. Her mother loved it, so after purchasing the property Barbara and her Mum relocated to their new home in Manakau. Her Mum died three years later, but Barbara is grateful to have spent this special time with her. Despite her multiple medical conditions Barbara said her Mum will always be remembered as being a "joyful person".

Following her mother's death, Barbara had planned to move back to Wellington, but due to her marriage breakdown, she decided to stay in Manakau. With limited accounting work available in the area, she reconsidered her employment options. Barbara had enjoyed caring for her mother and knew she had transferrable skills. Making the decision to stay in her home, she initially took on a role with Manawatū Accommodation and Sheltered Housing (MASH), caring for those physically and mentally challenged. Later, she worked a permanent night shift at a Rest Home for the elderly in Levin, but unfortunately had to step down from this role when she sustained a leg injury and couldn't walk without crutches. Barbara underwent surgery six months later and was unable to return to her previous job.

Contemplating 'where to from here' Barbara saw an advertisement for Adult Literacy Tutors. Intrigued, she investigated what was involved and found the work appealed to her. Appreciating that 'it's never too late to learn' she trained as an Adult Literacy and Numeracy Tutor when she turned 60 years of age. When she qualified, she taught reading and maths with people from all walks of life through the Horowhenua Adult Literacy Centre (HLC) where she worked for ten years. In this role she developed strong lasting friendships with fellow tutors and board members (known as 'Hals Angels') who she still meets up with on a monthly basis to this day.

In semi-retirement Barbara, who is now 72 years of age, is integral to the community in which she lives and works. She does an enormous amount of voluntary work in the Horowhenua. It's a portfolio lifestyle that she has built up over several years. Barbara does the accounts for Prisoners Aid and Rehabilitation, and the accounts (and is also a mentor) for 'Super Grans', (now known as 'Skills for Living'). She provides mentoring and accounting services to those that seek help. She is the Treasurer for the 'Waiopehu Women's Institute', the 'Horowhenua Arts Society' and the '60's Up Movement'. Furthermore, Barbara has a fabulous teddy bear collection, a life-long interest that was triggered with the tiny traditional

German teddy bear she was given for her christening by her godmother.

Barbara is on the committees for a cake decorating group, the 'Girl Guide Trefoil Guild' and 'Jack Allen House Drop-in Centre'. She also works at the local Citizens Advice Bureau, 'Horowhenua Sugarcraft' and every Wednesday she teaches knitting at Jack Allen House.

Like her parents, Barbara is very down to earth and appreciates diversity and inclusion. She draws on all of her skills all of the time and is never afraid to learn something new and lend a hand. Family is very important to her. She is very proud of her four children and two grandchildren, who all live in New Zealand, and she spends time with them whenever she can.

In her spare time, Barbara belongs to a craft group, a movie group and a coffee morning group and enjoys monthly bus trips with the '60's Up Movement'. All in all, she keeps herself busy and says, "Life is good". Her motto is "Every day above the ground is a good day; use it wisely and enjoy it".

Barbara's father

Barbara with her older brother Arthur in the back row.
Her younger siblings Cecil and Dorothy are sitting in front.

Barbara (on the far right of the photo), with her family celebrating her
parent's 25th Wedding Anniversary at the Skyline Restaurant in Wellington.

Barbara with her siblings and their respective partners and children

Barbara in the centre of this photo taken with her adult children and
grandchildren.

Barbara McGowan

HOHI JONES

Hohi is one of those people who radiates positivity, has a bubbly personality and an optimistic outlook on life and believes, 'we are the person we are today from our experiences'. Her earliest memory is as a pre-schooler when she had whooping cough. During her illness she remembers lying by the open fire while her parents and her older sister Kataraina took care of her. Hohi's father, who she adored, was a sharemilker in the rural community of Paengaroa where they lived. Hohi and her sister were the only two Māori girls at Paengaroa School, but they grew up in a world where "it wasn't good to be Māori". They weren't allowed to speak Māori, not even at home, and were strongly encouraged by their parents to 'follow the Pākehā way to fit in and be successful'. One of Hohi's most vivid memories of school was when the teacher asked, 'what are people called who live in New Zealand?' Hohi's response was "human-beings" and everyone in the class laughed. Embarrassed, she didn't know why they were laughing, and was mortified when the incident was printed in the school magazine. From that day forward she said she didn't feel as though she could speak up again and subsequently became quite shy around other people.

Hohi was the baby in the family until she was 12 years old, when her parents adopted a baby son, Tiata, to take on the family name. They later adopted her elder sister Kataraina's baby named James, who was born when Kataraina was only 14 years old and still in college. Growing up Hohi aspired to be a teacher when she left school, but Hohi's father was a very protective parent. He wanted Hohi and her siblings to stay with the family on the farm where they belonged. Things changed when her grandfather became ill. Hohi, who was 15 years old at the time and still at college, was asked to go and look after her grandfather who lived in Kaikohe in the Far North District of New Zealand. In those days young people did as they were told by their elders without question, so she left school and left home to live and care for her grandfather. While taking care of her grandad she secured a new job as a secretary for Hardie Bros, a carrying company, and earned the grand sum of five pounds, seven shillings and six pence per week. Hohi later got a job with the Post Office in Kaikohe where she worked as a teller.

Hohi loved her grandfather and enjoyed the time they spent together. Reflecting back on those days Hohi said she knew she was "a privileged child". For her 21st birthday she accompanied her grandfather to Hawaii for two weeks where he donated a canoe to a Polynesian village on the island of Oahu. Hohi said her grandfather, "was a Chief in his own time" and to this day she treasures her memories of him.

When her grandfather died, Hohi requested a job transfer to the Manners Street Post Office in Wellington. As an employee, she was also able to obtain a temporary place to live in one of the Post Office hostels. Relocating from the Far North to the capital city at the other end of the North Island was an extremely exciting step for a young person, as Wellington in those days was perceived to be "the big smoke". Life in the city was so different to the life she had experienced in Kaikohe. There were so many people and so many things to do, including lots of dances. It was at one of the dances that Hohi met Lafu, a young Samoan guy. Over time they became a couple, and she proudly sent a photo of her beau home to her family.

As the Easter break approached, Hohi's father asked her to come home and spend the holiday with the family, which she did. When she got home, her father had arranged for her to meet William, a nice young Māori man and his parents who were friends of the family. Afterwards her parents were keen to hear what she thought of William and asked if she liked him – to which Hohi responded 'yes' he was a nice young man. The conversation escalated to a new level when Hohi's parents suggested that she and William get married explaining that 'it's best to marry a person when you like each other, and then the relationship grows like a tree'. In hindsight Hohi said she must have been quite naive because the wedding plans were agreed and finalised during that Easter weekend in April, without any real discussion about her relationship and feelings for Lafu. The wedding in Kaikohe was scheduled to take place two months later in June, as this is when the milking stopped for the season enabling everyone to attend. Her parents wanted her to stay with them until the wedding, but against her parents' wishes Hohi insisted on returning to Wellington to resign from her job at the Post Office and work out her notice. She also wanted to meet with Lafu again, explain the situation to him, and end the relationship. Family ties were strong in both the Samoan and Māori culture. It was an exceedingly difficult situation for both of them, and a miserable parting of the ways.

Heartbroken, Hohi honoured the agreement she had made with her family and returned home. Her anxiety about the forthcoming wedding increased within the next few weeks when she realised, she was pregnant with Lafu's baby. Distraught given the wedding was imminent, she confided in her sister and a friend, but neither were very sympathetic to her predicament. Hohi decided to come clean with William and give him the opportunity to call off the wedding, but rather than end the relationship, he said he would take the baby on as his own. The wedding went ahead as planned on 3rd June 1965 – but Hohi said she knew in her heart it was wrong. Days after the wedding, while the newlyweds were on their honeymoon, Hohi took off back to Wellington. The days that followed were incredibly stressful for everyone concerned. Hohi's father, who meant everything to her, persuaded her to give the marriage a go for a few months. She was torn between what she wanted in her heart and honouring her father's wishes. Although Hohi did go back to William and try to give the marriage a go, at the end of the day it was Lafu she loved, and not William, so she walked away from the marriage.

Hohi returned to Wellington and eventually she was reunited with Lafu, her soulmate. They made a home together and had three sons. They finally got married in 1972. Just one year later, Lafu contracted chickenpox, serious complications set in and he developed pneumonia. Sadly, he died, aged 32. Heartbroken, Hohi a widow at 30, was left to raise her three boys then aged, one, four and seven, as a single parent. Lafu's family were very supportive. When they came over from Samoa for the funeral, they offered to take her three young children back to Samoa to live with them. Given the circumstances, Hohi allowed her eldest son to go to Samoa for six months to be with his Samoan family and experience their culture. When she and the other children visited him at Christmas, she brought him back home to New Zealand. As one would expect, this was a very challenging time for the family, but Hohi adopted a positive mindset and looked toward the future. Reflecting on this time in her life she said her motto was to 'enjoy what you have right now and be grateful', and this is the approach she took to raising her children.

Following her husband's death Hohi built a family home in Ascot Park, Porirua and in 1977, she and her sons moved in to start a new chapter of their life together. Around this time, she had joined a solo parent's group, and this is where she met her future husband, an Englishman named Ken Jones. Ken had two boys of his own and they and Hohi's boys got on well together. The relationship blossomed and in 1979, Ken and Hohi were married. The years sped by as they tend to for all of us when working and raising a family. Hohi's children grew up into fine strapping young men and she ensured they all got the best high school education she could offer. The three boys loved catching the train into Wellington each day to go to college where they developed life-long friendships with the mates they still have today.

In 1995, Ken was given the opportunity to take early retirement from his job as a Radio Officer on the Wellington - Picton ferries. By this time, their family home in Ascot Park was mortgage free, and the couple had a second home in Ōtaki. Thinking about their future in retirement, Ken and Hohi sold their home in Porirua and relocated to their Ōtaki residence. This gave them the chance to enjoy a more relaxed lifestyle, play golf with their friends, and take trips overseas. The transition into retirement went well and the couple happily settled into the Ōtaki community. Over the next 17 years they enjoyed life on their own terms and developed many new friendships. In 2011, Ken began to experience back pain and was referred for an MRI scan. Recalling the incident Hohi said, "everything happened very quickly when he was hospitalised and diagnosed with cancer", and he died suddenly in March 2011, aged 68 years.

Hohi and Ken had been happily married for 32 years. As a couple they had enjoyed life together raising their boys. They had also embraced retirement and the opportunities this phase of their life offered. Only three months prior to Ken's death they had enjoyed a wonderful family holiday together, for which Hohi is very thankful.

When Ken died, Hohi was grief stricken. Bereft, life seemed empty, and in the months that followed she became increasingly distressed and isolated. One day, when she was alone at home a friend named Malcolm rang her and asked how she was doing. Angry about her loss and her situation she let off steam with a big rant describing how lonely she was without Ken. To his credit Malcolm listened to Hohi. Then he asked her what she was doing about it. Her response was "nothing", which she said shocked her when she heard herself say it. Malcolm encouraged her to talk to a trusted neighbour about how she felt, without delay. As soon as she finished her phone call, Hohi took Malcolm's advice and approached her neighbour, explaining how she felt. The neighbour was only too pleased to listen, and this was to be a turning point in the grieving cycle for Hohi. Through these conversations Hohi said she realised she was a 'pack animal' – she's a very social person who needs the company of others, and this is what was missing in her life at that point in time. She understood she needed to take responsibility for herself and take action to change her situation. Hohi is so grateful to have had these conversations. She has never forgotten the support she was given by her friend and neighbour when she needed it most.

Acknowledging her life had changed, it was time to move on and look toward the future. In 2012, she made the radical decision to sell her Ōtaki home along with everything in it and make a fresh start. Keeping only her dog and her car she visited her adult children who were raising families of their own in other parts of the country, but she had no intention of becoming dependent on them.

When she returned to the Horowhenua to visit a friend she noticed an advertisement for an open day at a Retirement Village in Levin. Inquisitive, she went along to have a look. Hohi hadn't considered living in close proximity with other residents in a Retirement Village and was impressed when she was shown around the facilities. When she viewed an empty one-bedroomed self-contained apartment, she was captivated with the possibility of making this her new home. Excited at the prospect, but not wanting to make a rash decision she asked a friend to accompany her when she went back to have a second look at it. Seeing the apartment for the second time with a friend, she could imagine herself living there and that's when she made the decision to buy it - a decision she has never regretted.

Hohi had to set up her apartment from scratch as she had either sold or given away all of her household possessions when she sold her Ōtaki home. She had to purchase furniture, linen, crockery – just about everything, so she and her friend went on a shopping expedition, and she enjoyed every minute of it. The great thing is Hohi made this decision herself, in her own time. The choice was hers and within a couple of weeks she moved into her new apartment, aged 70. At the time of writing Hohi has lived here for eight years and she 'really likes it'. In her words, "there are always people to see, as the community is all around you so you can have company when you want it".

Despite the many challenges she has experienced over the decades, Hohi has retained her zest for life, embraces an attitude of gratitude, and leads an active social life both inside and outside the village. She is a vital personality in the village community's activities including the resident's birthday celebrations and dinners. In addition, she is a member of Grey Power, Breathe Easy, a Senior Citizens Group, the local Music Society, the Johnsonville Spiritual Group, and she is a member of three Country Music Clubs (Foxton, Levin, and Porirua). What's more she still keeps in touch with her friends in Ōtaki, Porirua, and Wellington. Hohi is immensely proud of her adult children, and her six grandchildren and constantly tells them how much they are loved. Although she is "always out and about", she makes exercise a priority and ensures she works through her home exercise regime every day to proactively manage her arthritis. Hohi said she tries hard to live by her own creed which is to, "love the person in the mirror every day. Become a person who is positive, cheerful and grateful for everything from morning to night". These principles are a great example of how we can embrace ageing and lead a happy, contented, and healthy life.

Hohi's grandfather, Hemi Whautere Witehira
(photo's from Hohi's private collection).

Hohi and Lafu

The Fa'amalepe whānau with Ken and Hohi Jones

Hohi and her three sons, Shaun on the right, Ralph and Jason on the left

JACOB CARROLL

Jacob was born and bred in the Bay of Islands, in the Far North District of the North Island of New Zealand. The bay has a natural harbour, numerous inlets and the area is considered to be one of the most popular fishing (especially big game fishing), sailing and tourist destinations in the country. As a teenager, Jacob was a boarder at St Peters Māori Boys College in Auckland (Te Kura Teitei o Hato Petera). In 1967, Jacob was 16 years old and it seemed that everything was changing. The world seemed smaller, friends were joining the military and leaving home to go to Vietnam, the music was different and New Zealand adopted decimal currency. Jacob had earned his School Certificate, was ready to leave school and looked towards his future, which for him was in New Zealand.

When he was growing up, the biggest employer in the Far North where Jacob lived was the Moerewa Freezing Works. The freezing works had a good reputation as a place to work; it provided year-round employment, the remuneration was excellent, and the organisation offered a career track for long-term employees. Jacob aspired to be a qualified butcher, so on leaving school he secured a job as a labourer at the works with the intention of working his way up the career ranks to achieve his goal. On starting work, he quickly learned that he could fast-track his training and experience if he transferred to the Ocean Beach freezing works in Bluff – a seaport town on the southern coast of the South Island. Although it was a long way from home (nearly 2,000 kilometres), Jacob decided to give it a go. After all, he loved travelling, wanted to see more of his own country, and he could achieve his goal of becoming a butcher sooner and reap the financial reward that came with this.

Jacob never regretted his decision to move to Bluff where he spent the next 10 years working his way up to become a butcher. His contract enabled him to work nine months of the year in Bluff and return to his hometown annually with all expenses paid by the company. Recalling that decade of his life Jacob said he "loved the job". In Bluff he had lots of experiences he wouldn't have had if he had remained in the Far North.

In the mid 1980's New Zealand experienced significant change in Government policy resulting in a profound effect on the watersiders, the railways, the freezing works and dairy factories. Several of the freezing works, including Ocean Beach, were closed and thousands of people were made redundant. Many of these people had excellent work records and had never been unemployed before. Nevertheless, when they applied for work elsewhere, they found that their previous skills and experience were considered to be irrelevant by prospective employers. By the time Jacob found himself in this situation, he was married with two young children to support. He applied for numerous jobs and became very disillusioned when recruiters didn't recognise his transferrable skills - for example organising, time management, communication, and teamwork skills. He realised he had experience in these areas but didn't have the qualifications required for the jobs that were available.

Jacob made the courageous decision to move to Wellington and go back to school. When he was much younger, he had wanted to be a social worker, so why not do that now? He researched what he needed to do and signed up to study at Victoria University. He also attended additional classes to build his confidence in using technology, as he'd had no exposure to computers when he was employed at Ocean Beach. Jacob said he "really struggled for the first three years at university" – but he "loved going back to school". This experience opened up a whole new world to him. He invested six years in his learning journey at Victoria University, graduating with a degree in Social Work, a qualification in Counselling, and he took further papers in psychology. He recalls that after he qualified prospective employers rang him to offer him a job – it wasn't the other way around. Jacob was also very clear on his career path – he wanted to work for community groups and Māori organisations, and this is where he has focused his time and energy ever since.

After leaving university Jacob managed a residential home for mental health patients in Porirua where he provided wrap-around support for patients who had been discharged into the community. Three years later he and his growing family moved to the Bay of Plenty to be nearer the wider whānau (family). Jacob secured a job in Whakatāne, doing similar work to what he'd been doing in Porirua, but on a bigger scale. This time he managed five residential homes for mental health patients in the local community and during this period Jacob's wife studied teaching. A couple of years passed, and the family had settled into the community when Jacob was asked to help facilitate the first year Counselling course at the local polytechnic. He was delighted to help out and thoroughly enjoyed the experience.

He developed further experience when he took a job at Tauranga Hospital working in the Māori Mental Health Forensic Unit. Looking back Jacob said it was a really rewarding role.

Reflecting on his career he said he "loves working in mental health". What he likes is to form a relationship with each individual and recognises what a privilege it is to care for people "who enter your world". Often, they have been directed by the Courts or the family. Jacob said he likes to regard mental health as an 'impairment' – a term that is less abrasive than 'mental health'. Describing the experience, he says "you share your space with each individual, and afterwards you leave them a totally different person, it's a privilege to be part of their journey to wellness – it's quite profound". Later in his career, Jacob became a lecturer/facilitator in social work, sociology and counselling with a Māori Health organisation in conjunction with the Manakau District Health Board. As a mental health therapist, Jacob has worked with patients across the health spectrum – patients in care, self-referrals and residential patients.

When Jacob retired from paid employment, he was approached to put his skills to use helping people working in health care to become qualified. He facilitated classes for students studying towards the achievement of the Community Support Workers Certificate, a requirement if they want to work with the District Health Board. At the time of writing Jacob is 67 years old. In later life he's had time to reflect. Thinking back, he remembered the major research project he completed in his last year at Victoria University. His project was entitled 'Suicide Aged' completed at a time when much of the focus was centred on youth suicide. He discovered that retirement for some is a major life event. Within a few months the feeling of loneliness can set in, especially if a life-long partner dies. Jacob found that with aged suicide, often people didn't read the signs – for example change in behaviour. Some people became withdrawn gradually or neglected to attend to basic needs such as personal hygiene, regular meals or attend to any medical conditions. Others resorted to stealing minor items of no consequence, for no apparent reason, when they had previously held a clean record all their lives. Loneliness has been identified as a huge problem in the older age group and Jacob suggests his research may be still relevant today.

Looking forward, Jacob wants to use his time in a positive way doing things he's always wanted to do, so he is working on his bucket list. He's always been a good pool and snooker player and enjoys a game with his friends at the Returned Services Association Club in Whakatāne. Jacob has always found the cue sport to be therapeutic and enjoys the camaraderie amongst his peers in practice sessions and at tournaments. This year he is honing his strategy and technique as his goal is to win a national competition. With this in mind he has joined two other clubs in neighbouring towns where he can meet his match with like-minded people across the spectrum of age groups and achieve his personal best.

The other big love of Jacob's life is his family. He has six adult children and loves to spend quality time with his 14 mokopuna (grandchildren) and two mokopuna nui (great grandchildren). What's more, they all live in New Zealand.

Jacob Carroll

Jacob's two youngest daughters Chevonn (on the left), Hine Miharo

Jacob with granddaughter Hilary Te Aro Mihirangi

Jacob with granddaughter Te Huinga

VALERIE PRATER

For as long as Valerie can remember she had always wanted to be a hairdresser. The fifth of eight children, Valerie was born and raised in Grove Park, London. Valerie's parents came from big families too, so there was always lots going on. Her Mum was a nurse and midwife, and her dad was a porter at the Seaman's Hospital in Greenwich before they were married, then he became a fireman based at a fire station in Bromley, Kent. Both parents encouraged their children to develop a good work ethic and follow their own path in life. It was a close family where everyone had the opportunity to speak up and have their say as long as they were respectful and listened to others' points of view when debating issues. Valerie found these skills to be invaluable as a teenager, when she started work as an apprentice hairdresser in Sydenham, London as she easily developed rapport with her co-workers and clients, a skill she maintains to this day. During these years she and her friends decided that one day they would all live somewhere else such as Ireland, Canada, America or perhaps New Zealand. Valerie had an uncle in New Zealand so knew quite a bit about the country, and what she knew appealed to her.

Valerie was 20 when she completed her apprenticeship. She married her fiancé Tony when she was 24 years old, and the couple moved to Kent where they started their family. Tony, a welder by trade, shared Valerie's desire to emigrate and so they made enquiries at New Zealand House in London to find out what they needed to do to fulfil this ambition under New Zealand's assisted passage immigration scheme. Valerie and

Tony's application to emigrate was accepted. On 1st March 1971, after a major strike in the United Kingdom, the Prater family boarded a plane at Heathrow Airport to come to New Zealand on assisted passage for ten pounds.

Initially the couple settled in Hamilton, where Tony had a job with Downers. A year later they moved to Rotorua, where Valerie worked part-time hairdressing. As Tony's welding skills were in high demand, during these years he was involved in big building projects at Kinleith, Kawerau and Wairakei. When Tony became part of the team that built the BNZ building on the corner of Lambton Quay and Willis Street in Wellington, the family moved to Newlands. By this time the couple's two children were both at school, so Valerie thought it was time to go back to work. Within a short period of time, she secured a hairdressing job at the James Hurst Salon in the Johnsonville Mall. Reflecting back on this experience Valerie said it opened up a whole new world of independence for her. She was earning a salary doing what she loved and enjoyed the daily interaction with her clients, many of whom remain good friends to this day.

Valerie made several major lifechanging decisions in the years that followed. When she and her husband parted ways, she took over the mortgages on their home in Wellington. Later, in partnership with a girlfriend, Valerie bought a salon called 'The Hairdresser'. The women worked hard over the years to build up the business and after a while Valerie took on the whole lease herself. Although Valerie was a very successful businesswoman, life wasn't all about work. She has always enjoyed exercise classes including Pilates and aerobics, walks regularly, is a keen gardener and enjoys reading. Importantly Valerie has kept in contact with her family in New Zealand and overseas.

Several family members, including her Mum and sisters have come out to visit her in New Zealand, and Valerie has made several trips back to England to spend fun times with family and friends. One of her sisters emigrated to Melbourne, Australia the same year that Valerie came to New Zealand so it's fairly easy to see each other on a regular basis.

When Valerie sold her hairdressing salon in Wellington, she stayed on as an employee, eventually retiring from paid work when she was 63 years of age. Throughout her life, hairdressing has been everything to her, so she maintains a keen interest and to this day, (17 years later), still services some of her clients, who have become lifelong friends, on a voluntary basis.

Valerie continued to pursue her exercise classes and other activities. She also joined a local Probus Club where she met new people and joined in the social activities. While Valerie enjoyed living in her two-story home in Wellington, she looked to the future and recognised that as she got older it was time for her to downsize and leave the hilly suburb. By this time, her adult son had moved to Brisbane. Her daughter and three grandchildren were living in Whanganui and several of her friends had moved to Levin in the Horowhenua, a town located less than 100 kilometres from both Wellington and Whanganui. Valerie often visited her friends in Levin and liked the feel of the place. She looked at several potential properties and found the perfect home close to the town centre. It was so convenient; she could walk to the shopping centre and her exercise classes. Looking ahead, she realised that if there came a time that she could no longer drive she would be OK. At 75 years of age Valerie made the decision to sell her house in Wellington and move to Levin. It was a good decision. Four years on she loves living in Levin where she is a member of several clubs, proactively manages her health and wellbeing and has developed a wide circle of friends – and she still does hairdressing for friends on a voluntary basis.

At the time of writing Valerie is fit and healthy at 79 years of age, as vivacious as ever, and continues to live life on her own terms. As she shared her story and reflected on her personal journey, she said she has 'no regrets'. She cherishes her family, including her son, daughter and three teenage grandchildren, and fondly remembers the close relationship she had with her Mum whom she said was 'the Bees Knees'. Valerie doesn't believe in living in the past - she lives in the present, makes the most of each day, and looks to the future. This year she is helping a friend with their decluttering project and there is plenty to look forward to. Luckily, just prior to the onset of the COVID-19 lockdown, Valerie's sisters came to visit her in New Zealand, and they were able to spend several joyful weeks of love and laughter together.

Valerie (on the far right) with her family on holiday

Valerie's Mum (centre front), and two of her sisters,
Marian and Pamela.

Valerie's sisters, from left to right Helen, Ann and Trisha

Valerie with her son John

Valerie with her daughter Suzanne and her grandchildren. From left to right, Ronan, Jordan, and Coral

PETER BLACKLER

Growing up on a small farm in Marton situated in the Rangitīkei district of New Zealand, Peter learned to do most things that needed doing. Apart from general farm work and gardening, he did all kinds of building and fencing work on the property. He was particularly interested in anything electrical or mechanical and remembers playing with old engines in the cow shed when he was a youngster. As a teenager he quickly learned how to refurbish them and discovered he could repair all kinds of machinery. On leaving school he followed his passion, trained as a radio technician, and completed an Electrical Engineering degree at Canterbury University.

In 1961, Peter started his first job with the Civil Aviation Administration of Air Department, the New Zealand government agency tasked with establishing the civil aviation system and infrastructure for New Zealand. Peter really loved the job and over the years he became very knowledgeable about the industry, had the opportunity to work in various roles, and held senior management positions. During this time, like other government agencies, Civil Aviation went through significant changes. In the 1970's and 80's the organisation became a standalone Department of Civil Aviation, then later the Civil Aviation Division of the Ministry of Transport. In 1987 the operational services of Air Traffic Control and Engineering were set up as a State-Owned Enterprise, known as the Airways Corporation of New Zealand. The regulatory sections of the Civil Aviation Division (Licensing, Certification, Safety Standards) remained as a Government service and eventually became the Civil Aviation Authority of New Zealand. Throughout these decades there were numerous restructures, and unfortunately in 1987, after 26 years of service Peter, as an Assistant Manager of the Engineering Division, was made redundant.   Peter has the distinction of being the first redundancy out of the Airways Corporation, three months after it was established and there were many more redundancies following Peter's departure. It was a very rough experience at the time but opened up other opportunities.

After a few weeks working on house alterations, Peter was offered a position with Cory Wright and Salmon in Wellington working on potential contracts for the New Zealand air traffic control system.   All was going well for a few months until the company was placed into receivership. Fortunately, Peter was very well known in the industry both on and offshore. Through the contacts established at Cory Wright and Salmon, he was subsequently offered a 12-month contract with an American/Canadian company, Thomson/Hickling, to be part of a team undertaking a review of the Canadian Air Traffic System. At the time Peter and his wife Christine had three teenage children and their family home in Island Bay, Wellington to consider. Talking it over with the family, Michael, Peter's eldest elected to stay in New Zealand and live in the family home. Peter's daughter, Stephanie aged 17 was about to commence a degree course at Massey University in Palmerston North and thought the Christmas holidays in Ottawa would be great. Their youngest daughter Penny, (then aged 12), was keen to move to Ottawa, so the decision was made for Peter to accept the contract and move to Canada.

After leaving New Zealand, the first six weeks were spent in Washington DC in the United States, while waiting for the appropriate visas to come through. The following 12 months were spent in Ottawa working on the project undertaking a review of the Canadian Air Traffic system. During this period, every opportunity was taken to explore the Canadian and North American towns, cities and countryside from Prince Edward Island in the East to Vancouver and Victoria in the West, and from Moosonee in the North to New York and Washington DC to the South. Peter has fond memories of lots of visits made through all of the seasons, the long warm evenings on the bike trails in summer, to well below freezing in winter, when they also enjoyed night skiing and ice skating.

On completion of the Canadian contract, Peter was offered another role with the Civil Aviation Authority in New Zealand, which he accepted. In this role Peter joined the small team re-writing all the aviation Safety Rules and Standards for New Zealand and before long he was appointed Manager of the Rules and Standards section. Peter also represented New Zealand at a number of International Civil Aviation Organisation Forums on aviation safety. After 16 years of developing and managing the aviation safety rules and standards, Peter realised he needed to achieve a better work / life balance and in February 2006 he formally retired to move into a part-time role as the Technical Manager for Rules and Standards. Although there was a big retirement farewell, Peter was scheduled to be back at the desk after four weeks away. This part time role (three days a week) was only intended to continue for a couple of years but eventually in February 2011 Peter finally closed up the Rule book, and at age 67 he moved into full time retirement – 50 years and one day after he first signed up with the Civil Aviation Administration. In effect, throughout his working life Peter has only been employed with two organisations – Civil Aviation in New Zealand and Thomson/Hickling in Canada.

Throughout his life Peter has always had projects on the go in his spare time. In addition to maintaining the family home in Wellington, he and Christine purchased a house in Waikanae on the Kāpiti Coast 20 years ago. The couple rented this property out when they were living in the city. Sixteen years ago, they sold the home they had lived in for 37 years in Island Bay and moved to Waikanae. In the year prior to moving to Waikanae Peter began renovating and extending the house at Waikanae – two bedrooms and a bathroom added on top of the house, a complete refurbishment and alteration of the original house area, and the whole area under the house excavated to provide 100 square metres of workshop and basement space. This building project was initiated while Peter was still working full time with Civil Aviation in Petone, so he regularly commuted by car between Island Bay, Waikanae, and Petone. When the cottage next door came up for sale, Peter purchased that too, and he and Christine lived in it for a year until the renovations of their family home had been completed. The cottage is now managed as a long-term homestay for overseas visitors on sabbatical breaks and other professionals.

Peter is also a long-time member of Wellington Vintage Machinery Incorporated, which is located in an old cheese factory in Upper Hutt. This non-profit charitable club was established for people, who like Peter, are interested in preserving and restoring vintage machinery. The club is virtually a museum with dozens of working engines including sawmill engines, tractors, a steam traction engine, and pre-decimal cash registers, and other household items from previous generations. Many of the machines have a particular historical significance to the Hutt Valley and Wellington areas and are lovingly restored and displayed for future generations to enjoy. Peter is the Treasurer of this club, which has a thriving membership and plenty of electrical and mechanical projects on the go. Over the 19 years he has been a member, funding has been raised to upgrade the kitchen and associated facilities, and to build a 150 square metre shed to accommodate the increasing stock of machinery and the tools required to restore them. Numerous funding applications have been made, and resource consents and building consents had to be obtained through the various channels before the vision for this club became a reality.

Over two decades, public displays have been held, and numerous group visits from senior citizens to schools and kindergartens have been coordinated and supervised, providing an opportunity for the community to see these machines restored to their former glory. A nostalgic trip for the older citizens and an opportunity for the children to learn about, and to have hands on experience with the machines and other things from their great grandparents' days. The Wellington Vintage Machinery Museum is a fabulous community asset, and a credit to the talented men who have spent countless hours on these projects. What a legacy!

In 2010, at the Easter market, a flyer about an upcoming public meeting in Waikanae caught Peter's eye.   The flyers were distributed by three local men, Nigel Clough, Andrew Stephens and Charles Lloyd, stating the philosophy and benefits of a Menzshed. The purpose of this not-for-profit organisation is to 'bring men together in one community space to share their skills, have a laugh, and work on practical projects either individually (for personal projects), or as a group for projects for the shed or for the community'. Nigel had previously belonged to the Wellington Menzshed and thought that a similar facility may be right for the Kāpiti Coast area. Nigel, Andrew, and Charles wondered if there were others in the community who would be interested. Peter went along to the public meeting to find out more. By the end of the meeting 27 men had signed up and paid the $10 membership fee, thus enabling the Menzhed Kāpiti to be registered as an Incorporated Society. Nigel became the first Chairman of Menzshed Kāpiti.

The first task was to find a suitable building in Kāpiti to get the Shed established. Nigel talked to the mayor and a local Councillor to help find a local building they could use. A small building at the Council's Works Depot in Waikanae was offered to the group for $1 a year rent. Although the building was 'pretty run down' the men quickly got together and cleaned it out.   The Council donated cable and the guys from the Menzshed dug the trenches on the site, installed the power and that was it, Menzshed Kāpiti was up and running with the aim of 'promoting the health and wellbeing of mainly retired and older men'. Initially between 10 and 12 men came each time they met. Once the word got around there was great support from the community and particularly from the women folk who wanted a place for their men to go for a few hours. Lots of tools and machines were donated from people downsizing and from widows cleaning out their husband's workshop. Bunnings, a hardware retailer, donated a gazebo so that the guys could have morning tea out of the weather. The building was full of tools and all sorts of other good bits that may be useful one day. Things went from there. As Peter said the shed is "a place where men do what men do". It's a place to 'socialise with like-minded men, to practice old skills, learn new ones, share know-how, pursue hobbies, enjoy company and give back to the community'.

As time passed the membership of the Menzshed Kāpiti grew, and with that more space was required to accommodate the men and their projects. In keeping with Peter's past involvement with community groups, he took on the role of Treasurer, and with his engineering and management experience he became the leader of site developments for the MenzShed. In 2012 the Council relocated their Works facilities to Paraparaumu, and this provided the opportunity for Peter to negotiate a 10-year lease with Council for Menzshed to take over an adjacent three-bay tractor shed. Considerable clean-up was required so the men quickly got to work utilising their skills and experience, and with the aid of a grant from the Waikanae Community Board and trailer loads of office furniture and fittings when Council relocated back to their refurbished offices in Paraparaumu, the facilities were upgraded with work benches, basic kitchen facilities, and a temporary toilet. As more people learned about the Menzshed, hand and power tools, wood, windows and other equipment were donated by local businesses and members of the community.

In 2013, various Menzsheds from around New Zealand held their first national conference in Nelson. At this conference they established the constitution and a set of rules to form a national body – called Menzshed New Zealand. Peter with his skills and experience played a key role in developing the constitution and rules and became the Treasurer. The second national conference was to be held in Kāpiti in 2014 and so better facilities were required at the Menzshed site. Peter consulted with the owners of neighbouring properties and the Council, and successfully obtained a Resource Consent and a Building Consent to build a veranda across the front of the sheds and to build an additional three bay shed. The local community board helped sponsor the national event, which was held at El Rancho, a local Christian Camp. Former Prime Minister, Jim Bolger, set the tone for the conference and more than 80 Menzshed members from around NZ attended this hugely successful event.

Since its inception, the Menzshed Kāpiti has gone from strength to strength. With the ever-increasing number of men coming to the Shed, it became apparent that more workshop space and better facilities were urgently needed. Morning tea and briefings outside under the veranda is great during the summer but not so good on a cold wet winter day. Over the past three years Peter has again consulted with neighbours, worked with engineers and architects, and with Council to obtain a Resource Consent and Building Consent to build additional facilities at the Waikanae site. At the time of writing funding has been raised, and the men at the Shed have commenced building the new facilities – 110m^2 of purpose-built kitchen, accessible toilets, office, and a large meeting area, with 40m^2 of covered deck across the front. Further construction in the next year will include 140m^2 of new workshop space. Peter has also worked with the Council to obtain a new 20-year lease for the MenzShed to continue its operations at the Waikanae site. In addition to the building and workshop activities, a number of the men have landscaped the site and developed very prolific gardens with a good supply of fresh vegetables going to the local foodbank.

The shed has 120 financial members with 45-60 guys showing up each Tuesday and Thursday to work on numerous personal, conservation and community projects in the well-equipped workshop, and to have a cuppa and a chat with one another. For Peter, one of the most significant projects they have worked on is the construction of white crosses identifying World War 1 (WW1) casualties, complete with names, numbers and poppy logos. These were installed in the 'Field of Remembrance' in the Botanic Gardens in Wellington, to commemorate the soldiers from the Wellington Region who died in battles during the first world war. Initially 500 crosses were assembled and sorted for Armistice Day in 2015. Another 964 memorial crosses were requested in 2016, 1500 crosses for 2017, and 1800 crosses for 2018. Menzshed members pulled together as a team on separate days when no other shed activities were operating to meticulously assemble the crosses, sort them into alphabetical order and pack into storage boxes that were also made at the Shed. They are a credit to our community, and a very moving experience to see all crosses (about 5,000) set out in the Botanical Gardens in 2018.

Clearly it takes considerable personal drive, research,

paperwork, consultation, fundraising, and sponsorship to establish and successfully maintain the Wellington Vintage Machinery Incorporated, the Menzshed Kāpiti, and the Menzshed New Zealand in collaboration with like-minded individuals. In Peter's words these are places "where men do what men do". The organisations bring men together to facilitate fellowship, instil a sense of purpose and community, share their ideas and skills and work on meaningful projects. Peter, as a member and as the Treasurer of these organisations has been instrumental in the establishment, growth and success of these community assets. Furthermore, he is also a member of the Waikanae Community Patrol.

Peter, now in his late 70's, lives with his wife Christine in their Waikanae home. The couple enjoy busy and fulfilling lives and appreciate family time with their three adult children and seven grandchildren. Peter's basement and workshop is also like a museum with a great collection of clocks, radios, gramophones, sewing machines, a vintage tractor, vintage machinery and engines, and other great bits and pieces that others may regard as junk. Peter just needs a few more hours in the day to work on the home projects and to get more of those clocks, radios and machines into working order.

For more information on:

Menzshed New Zealand see www.menzshed.org.nz

Menzshed Kāpiti see www.menzshedKāpiti.org.nz

Wellington Vintage Machinery Incorporated see
https://uhcl.recollect.co.nz/nodes/view/14761

A 1952 Massey Harris Pony tractor
Peter stripped it down to the last nut and bolt and then re-built it.

Peter's first major engine restoration. A before and after photo
of the A 1920 Lister L engine

Morning tea at Kāpiti Menzshed

The current building project at Kāpiti Mezshed

The ANZAC crosses in the 'Field of Remembrance' in the Botanical Gardens

Peter Blackler

Some of the items Peter has restored in his basement.

A sample of Peter's collection of clocks and vintage machinery

RICHARD LEACH

In semi-retirement, Richard is a self-employed accountant and business coach who encourages his clients to achieve their dreams. For the first 50 years of his life he lived in Christchurch, the largest city in the South Island, where he went to school. In those days, all young men in New Zealand were required to complete 13 weeks compulsory military training when they turned 18.   When Richard was conscripted, he went to Burnham Camp to undertake his basic and core training, and as he had been a cadet with St John, it was a natural progression for him to go into the Medical Corps. Returning to civvy street after he had fulfilled his military service, he maintained his membership and service with St John and trained as a primary school teacher.

Although Richard enjoyed teaching, he was keen to expand his skills and experience, take on additional work and generate additional income to supplement the family's budget. Richard's stepbrother Ken was a knitting machine engineer with a local clothing manufacturer called Lane Walker Rudkin that was always looking for night-shift knitters (midnight-8am). Richard applied for and secured a job as a sock knitter at night. Exposure to the manufacturing industry peaked Richard's interest in business so he looked for other opportunities to get hands on experience. Before long he got a job as a salesclerk with Crown Crystal Glass, New Zealand glass manufacturers and while working there he met the firm's accountant. In these conversations Richard soon realised that he had little understanding of the financial aspects of running a business and made up his mind to rectify this and get a business degree. While getting married and raising his family Richard studied for his degree on a part-time basis and qualified as an Accountant – a profession he found extremely rewarding. Nevertheless, Richard has always been inquisitive about business and wanted to know as much as he could about the different aspects of it, so he completed a Diploma in Management, Marketing and Business Planning and began coaching owner/operators of small businesses who were struggling as they didn't have the business skills themselves.

Over the years Richard was also an active member of several not-for-profit organisations in the Christchurch community. He was a member of St John from 1948-2000, Secretary for the Christchurch Council for the Handicapped for three years, and Treasurer for the Canterbury/Westland Baptist Association. He was also a member of the Labour Party for a long time. Richard was the Chairman of the Epilepsy Association and has been a member of both the Hearing Association and the Stroke Group, and he has been a Justice of the Peace for nearly 50 years!

When the economic downturn hit, Richard was made redundant. He applied for 204 jobs before becoming totally disillusioned, when quite by chance a Rawleigh representative came to the house. Rawleigh's medicinal products are sold directly to the public through an established network of local distributors. When the Rawleigh Healthcare representative came to the house Richard outlined his situation, explaining that he had no job and no money to buy the products on offer. Listening to Richard's story and recognising his business, sales and marketing experience, the representative suggested to

Richard that he could take over his old Rawleigh's distribution route as he already had more clients than he could manage in his new route. Richard accepted the dealership proposal.

Richard continued to apply for other employment opportunities and was offered a role with a firm in Levin. It was an opportunity, so he accepted the position and he and his wife sold their Christchurch home and relocated from the South Island to the Horowhenua in the North Island. Disappointingly this job only lasted nine months. Undeterred, Richard secured another job, this time as a Cost Accountant with Avalon Television Studios in Lower Hutt, and so began the daily 180 kilometres return trip from Levin to work each day.

Richard worked at Avalon Studios for six years. Meanwhile, he and his wife Fay joined the Assembly of God Church and established themselves in their new community. Fay took over his Rawleigh's dealership in Levin and Richard began to undertake some freelance work for small businesses in the Horowhenua as an Accountant. He also joined the Accountant's and Taxation Institute of New Zealand (ATAINZ). Twelve years sped by and Richard, who is now semi-retired, provides business, accounting, taxation, and compliance expertise to more than 80 clients. Richard loves his work and is making a welcome contribution to the business community, especially small and medium-sized businesses that are experiencing difficulties. Instead of slowing down in later life, Richard is energised and passionate about growing his business and still finds time to assist not-for-profit organisations meet their business requirements.

Richard leads a very active life. He has always been interested in star gazing and was the Secretary for the Foxton Beach Astronomical Society for three years. New Zealand, with its limited pollution and clear skies is the perfect haven for this hobby. He is the Treasurer for Levin and District's Senior Citizens Association Inc. Richard said he has always maintained a healthy diet and exercises regularly. Since moving to Levin, he and his wife joined a gym, took up weight training and they walk several kilometres most days, and as a result they enjoy a healthy lifestyle. A keen dancer, over the years Richard has done ballroom, folk and square dancing and now includes Israeli dancing as part of his exercise routine.

Now 84 years of age, Richard embraces longevity and looks forward to the future and what this may bring. Quoting from the Bible, Genesis 6.3, Richard notes than man could live for 120 years and jokes that, "he may claim additional years for good behaviour". Richard really does exemplify the 'you are as young as you feel' adage. He laughingly said, "when I turn 122 years of age, I'll ask the Minister of Finance for a pay rise"! At the time of writing Richard and his wife have five grandchildren and 12 great-grandchildren.

To learn more about the services Richard provides for his clients check out his website https://achievinglifestyles.co.nz/

Richard Leach

MARGARET PULLAR

Margaret's ancestors, the McCarrolls, were from Northern Ireland. In 1864, Margaret's Great Grandfather John, two of his sons, and his eldest daughter Mary, came to New Zealand. His eldest son - Margaret's grandfather, Robert McCarroll, came to New Zealand a year later, bringing his mother and younger siblings with him. Robert, who was engaged to be married at the time, was an accountant and represented All Ireland as their soccer goalkeeper. He intended to immediately return to Ireland but never did.

The McCarrolls opened a shop selling Irish linen goods in Auckland. To this day, Margaret treasures and uses the family's beautiful linen tableware she has inherited. When the family shifted north, they became the first Pākehā settlers at Mareretu, in the Kaipara District of Northland. The McCarroll Brothers became kauri bushmen, sheep, and cow farmers. Robert also used his accountancy skills to assist other pioneers. He eventually settled in the family's homestead on the original block of land they purchased. Interestingly, the very last gap in New Zealand's North Island main trunk railway, known as McCarrolls' Gap, was not completed until after 1923.

As children, Margaret and her two younger brothers learnt to swim in Kikiwiti stream by their home. They played on the steep hills, in the native bush, in the creeks and on the stumps of the huge kauri trees that were felled on the hill behind their home to build the original homestead. The many floods also created great adventures. Margaret recalls the most significant people in her early life and primary school years, apart from her parents and grandparents, were the old Waiapo couple. The Waiapo couple and their two daughters lived beside the school boundary fence on public land alongside a clay track. Clarki was Mr Waiapo's nickname. In those times it was standard practice to call a wife by her husband's Christian name – hence Mrs Waiapo was known as Mrs Clarki. One of their daughters looked after Margaret and Margaret's two younger brothers when they were preschoolers. This enabled Margaret's mother Betty (nee Aikman) and Clarki to do the milking when Margaret's father Reg, an excellent shearer, was absent shearing on neighbouring farms. Margaret remembers the Kuia Waiapo (the older woman) always made her welcome in her manuka brush roof and Punga walled whare (home). She recalls spending many hours there sitting beside her wood-burning range, being permitted the privilege of sweeping the Kuia's earth floor with her manuka brush broom. Margaret also has fond memories of helping Mrs Clarki tend her vegetable garden and tasty strawberry patch.

Margaret was five when she began her formal education at the tiny Mareretu sole charge school. She recalls there were only 12 children at the school, and never more than 20 in the years she attended. Her earliest school memory was when she got into trouble with the teacher for spending her lunchtimes leaning over the boundary fence talking to the Kuia and her daughter. She said she could not understand why she was no longer allowed to talk to the Waiapos who had been a big part of her life. A bit of a schemer, Margaret climbed a gum tree on the fence line so she could talk to them without being seen.

Unfortunately, she climbed too high and could not get down - the bell went – she was literally stuck up a gum tree! Thankfully, the Kuia's daughter, whose name was Wiki, helped her down, but Margaret was late for the afternoon class and again got into trouble!

At school, Margaret saw firsthand what Māori valued and how Māori were discriminated against. Their Tapu (sacred place) of the open grave, hewn into rocks within the native bush bounding the McCarroll's family farm. Their love of eeling and swimming. Their suffering of glue ear, body sores, and hair lice. Being called derogatory names. The severe punishment Māori children received for speaking Māori at school - at a time when that was not permitted.

Margaret was the first female from Mareretu to attend secondary school. In her first year, she took correspondence. It was the year in which the polio epidemic began. The following year, to get to school, she remembers catching a goods train at six am each morning. It had travelled overnight from Auckland, with two carriages at its rear. Her companions were six Māori girls who got on at the next three stations along the line. All the girls sat, talked, and did their homework together. Back then, they were practicing co-operative and mastery learning without even realising it. When they got off the train in Whangārei, the teenagers had to walk for a further 30 minutes to get to Whangārei Girls High School. They returned to the station at three-thirty pm to catch the train home again. Margaret made this four-hour train trip every day, Monday to Friday, each week during term time for one year.

The following year, she boarded in Whangārei - travelling up by train on Mondays and returning on Fridays. At a social function, when alcohol had unexpectedly loosened the tongue of one of the Māori girls, Margaret recalls being told bluntly and uncharacteristically of the hidden feelings of antipathy, resentment and sense of dispossession felt deep down by one of her train companions towards "You Pākehā!" (foreign white person). It was an experience she has never forgotten.

Margaret enjoyed school and did well. In the fifth form, competing against girls in the more senior forms, she was delighted to win the Whangārei Girls High School's senior speech contest and cup. A month before her 17th birthday, she began to train as a Home Craft Teacher at Auckland Teacher's College. She was in the first group to be trained as secondary school teachers in this subject outside of Dunedin. Accordingly, she and her colleagues were placed in 'Section R' with university graduates who were completing their teacher training year. The theory was that their shared experience with university graduates would help them learn to behave and communicate appropriately with staff who were far more senior than they were and with considerably more education!

After completing her teaching qualification, Margaret taught Home Economics at District High Schools in Howick, Papakura, and Helensville -a term at each. Then two years at Te Awamutu College, followed by one year at Whangārei Girls High School. The presbyterian minister at Te Awamutu suggested that, as she was their senior bible class leader, she should attend the Presbyterian Church Youth Conference in Palmerston North. It was at this conference that Margaret met her future husband Gordon who was a farmer from Southland. The couple married two years later in 1957. Margaret fondly remembers putting her Home Economics training into action by designing and making her wedding gown as well as making and icing her wedding cake.

After the wedding, Margaret moved to Southland to live on the sheep and grain farm that Gordon's Trapski-Pullar family had already owned for three generations. In the first few years, Margaret delighted in making several wedding gowns, icing wedding cakes, and teaching young women to sew their clothes. For the next 42 years, she thoroughly enjoyed Southland farming life. During the late fifties and the sixties, she and Gordon had four children: Phillip, Karen, Bronwyn, and Logan.

In the late 1960s and early 1970s, Margaret led a successful and lively Church Youth Group of 16 to 20year olds. Although it's now been well over 50 years since Margaret facilitated the Pukerau Group, members of that group still keep in touch and visit her.

In 1973, Margaret and her husband spent a week attending Interchurch Personal Growth Training in Wellington. That made a significant positive influence on their lives. While there, they met Reverends Evan Sherrard, and Robin Lane, who had undertaken Clinical Pastoral Education (CPE) Training in the United States; and Reverend Neal Brown, who had undertaken his CPE training in Australia. Valued lifelong relationships were formed.

As a consequence of her work with the Youth Group, Margaret was invited on several occasions to join the Presbyterian Christian Education Staff for their annual national week of 'In-Service Training'. She also undertook extensive Bible Study; Eldership Study; Human Relations and Gestalt Training at Cameron Centre, Dunedin; also, Gestalt Therapy with Don Kapperick - who was travelling through Gore at that time. Margaret was one of the first three women elders ordained in Pukerau Parish and served on several Presbytery and National church committees.

Over time, members of the Pukerau Youth Group asked Margaret to teach their parents what she was teaching them. Reflecting on the prospect, Margaret decided to become a Marriage Guidance Counsellor and began training in 1974. In later years she was appointed a Supervisor of Marriage Guidance Counsellors. Margaret was elected to a national committee for what later became 'New Zealand Relationship Services' where she was responsible for interviewing and selecting supervisors for them from the Waitaki River, south. In 1993 the Southland Branch of Relationship Services awarded Margaret Life Membership of their organization.

Throughout Margaret's life she has never been afraid to break new ground and, as a result, is a pioneer in her own time. She was the first woman to serve on the Gore High School Board of Governors. In 1974 she became secretary for a small group of community and church leaders from Eastern Southland and

West Otago who sought to establish a Counselling Centre in Gore (like the Cameron Centre in Dunedin). At the time, the only other Counselling Centres in New Zealand were in Auckland and Tauranga. In 1977, the Gore and Districts Community Counselling Centre opened in Gore. The Reverend Don Fergus, a New Zealand Presbyterian Minister, and qualified Clinical Pastoral Supervisor, was the first Director at the helm. Forty-four years later the Centre is still providing an excellent service for the community. What an achievement!

Eager to take the next step, Margaret commenced training as a psychotherapist. She believes that receiving quality personal psychotherapy and skilled supervision are two essential factors in effective psychotherapy training. In 1978 she began studying extramurally for a degree in Psychology. She obtained full membership of the New Zealand Association of Psychotherapy (NZAP) in 1985. She was the first person to go through their new membership process of writing three case studies, as well as being personally interviewed. Two years later, she graduated from Massey University with a Bachelor of Arts in Psychology and Sociology.

Further part-time Psychotherapy training commenced in 1988 to meet the requirements for a three year Post Graduate Diploma from The Australia and New Zealand Association of Psychotherapy (ANZAP) in 1991. An additional year of Supervisor training from this organisation followed.

Margaret then became the Director of the Gore Counselling Centre, a role she held for 11 years. A highlight during this time was an invitation to present a paper, about the Gore Centre and its work in a rural area, at the Australasian Mental Health Conference in Sydney. Margaret, along with psychiatrist Peter McGeorge, and a small group of New Zealanders, also taught their Australian counterparts at the conference aspects of Māori Tikanga (customs and traditions), for example, appropriate welcomes and Waiatas (Māori songs that convey particular messages).

Margaret retired from the Gore Centre in 1998 when she was 65 years old. After 42 years of farm life through both good times and the tough times, she and her husband Gordon shifted from "Crichton Park" to Gore. However, retirement was not on her agenda. Instead, Margaret established and managed her part-time private practice for the next 10 years. During these years she was asked to assess professional clinical papers submitted for Membership of the New Zealand Association of Psychotherapists. She also participated in the oral assessments of these candidates. Margaret recalls this work as being both a privilege and a challenge. In recognition of her service as a psychotherapist, she was awarded the Association's Distinguished Service Award in 2008 at a special event held in the Māori meeting house on Te Tii Marae at Waitangi – it was an enormous honour!

Margaret and Gordon had been married for almost 60 years when he died in 2015, just before his 90th birthday. The couple had worked together as a team raising their four children, in the garden, and on the farm. Gordon worked upon, and managed the farm business, while Margaret clothed and fed the family, and cared for the live-in farm workers. She also provided all the catering for visiting agents, shearing, tailing, haymaking, and the harvesting business. Throughout their marriage, Gordon had always been hugely supportive and encouraged Margaret to pursue her interests. Gordon "was also absolutely marvelous at cooking breakfast each morning".

Gordon's Nuffield Scholarship in 1962 gave Gordon and Margaret worldwide experiences and contacts that greatly influenced their lives. Apart from his practical farming, the grain harvesting and drying businesses, Gordon was involved (especially during the 1960s, 1970s and 1980s) in Young Farmers, Federated Farmers, rural and national politics, the church, and community organisations. He served as a Justice of the Peace, and a celebrant at funerals and weddings. His activities also put demands upon Margaret, who frequently acted as his secretary, editor, and companion.

Margaret, now 86 years of age, has been a widow for five years. She lives in Gore where she cares for her large garden. She has been and continues to be, an integral member of Gore's community. Her current project is the development of the historic Pukerau Cemetery that opened in 1880. As secretary of the Pukerau Cemetery Support Group Trust, she is working with the community to develop the cemetery into an attractive peaceful historical centre. A kiosk will honour the district's ancestors and those who have served at war. Steps are underway to also identify and mark the unmarked graves, enhance access, and improve landscaping.

Reflecting on her life experience, Margaret said that over the years she has learnt that when you have an idea or are working towards a groundbreaking goal, 'breakthroughs happen immediately after the opposition is at its greatest'. She has found that 'it's important not to give up, as the achievement of an idea is just around the corner'. Margaret's past achievements and her vision and work is a testament to this.

Throughout her life, Margaret has loved tramping as a relaxation. In recent years she has appreciated unique experiences such as geological group trips with Hamish Campbell to the Chatham Islands and New Caledonia, and trips to Europe and Taiwan with her daughters. She thoroughly enjoys and values contact with her four adult children, their spouses, six grandchildren and five great-grandchildren. They all live in New Zealand. In 1995, Margaret wrote "The McCarroll Family History" circulating copies within the extended family. In 2013, Margaret published a very well-received book she had written, "Carse Head & Crichton Park Farms: A story of the land and its people", the Trapski–Pullar family. Photographs included throughout illustrate farming developments, and unintentionally, a delightful portrayal of southern clothing styles over a hundred and thirty-nine years. The fifth and sixth generation in the Trapski-Pullar family now live on, and farm, "Crichton Park" - the family property.

Margaret and Gordon

Margaret tramping in Stewart Island

Logan, Phillip, Bronwyn, Karen, Margaret, and Gordon

Margaret with her great-grandson Remi

"People will not look forward to posterity who never look back to their ancestors." - Edward Burke.

DAWN McCORMICK

Dawn, a fun-loving spirited individual with a zest for life celebrated her 95th birthday in Whanganui surrounded by family and friends. The youngest of two children, she was born in 1925, in Ōtāne, a small rural settlement in Hawkes Bay on the east coast of the North Island of New Zealand. Dawn and her older brother, Earl Roy (who was always known as Roy), were raised in a very loving family environment, with extended family living nearby. Dawn's father, Stan Mudgway, had a shop in Ōtāne where he made furniture. In his spare time, he was a member of the local acting society and regularly organised plays for the community. He was also very musical, enjoyed singing and played the accordion. Dawn recalls that from the age of five she would dress up and sing all the old songs with him. Performing in concerts together, they were often asked to entertain, an activity they both relished.

In the grip of the Great Depression of the 1930's, work was scarce and there was mass unemployment in New Zealand. Times were tough and many families struggled to cope. In January 1931, Dawn's father had the chance to build the grandstand at the Taradale Racecourse 50 kilometres away from home. It was a welcome opportunity, but it was too far away in those days to commute backwards and forwards to work on a daily basis. As it was summertime in New Zealand, the family relocated to Taradale and set up home in two tents on the racecourse so they could all stay together. Dawn vividly remembers erecting the tents and the whole family collected wood to feed the great big copper which was used to heat the water to cook their food and wash their clothes. It was a big adventure for the children and Dawn was going to attend Green Meadows School when the new school year started.

On 3rd February 1931, Dawn and her mother, Lucy (nee Lester), caught the early bus into Napier to do some shopping. Roy, who was 11 years older than Dawn, and very independent, cycled into Napier on his bike with one of his friends. It was a hot sunny day and the family planned to meet up later in the day to go swimming at the pool in Napier. Dawn said, "when we got off the bus, we were looking in the window of Hannah's shoe shop when my mother felt the first shake and shouted get to Mummy, get to Mummy!" The massive earthquake with a magnitude of 7.8 violently shook for two and a half minutes. Dawn said, "it seemed to go on forever, we were thrown apart like puppets and couldn't stand up. Glass was shattering all around us". Dawn's mother tried to hold on to her as buildings started to collapse all around them. Within minutes "there were several more shakes, it was very noisy and very frightening". Recalling the experience Dawn said, "a man shouted to us and told us to go straight to Clive Square as quickly as we could". Swaying and rocking amidst the shakes Dawn and her mother along with others, hurried to the safety of Clive Square, a park area situated a short distance away from the crumbling buildings in the shopping centre. "Then the fires started and there was no water", as the water supply had been disrupted by the earthquake. Chaos ensued as nearly all the buildings around them were levelled.

The Napier earthquake devasted the Hawkes Bay region, killing 256 and injuring thousands of people. Feeling the shakes,

Dawn's father got in his car and took off to find his family but turned back to get planks of wood and their kayaks when he saw the extent of the damage of the road and the bridges. He must have been frantic as he drove as far as he could around the rubble of the collapsed buildings and when he could go no further, he kayaked down the streams to get to Napier. During the day Clive Square had become a meeting place and Roy, who had been knocked off his bike during the earthquake, was reunited with Dawn and his mother. Dawn said, "we were in Clive Square all day. It was 4.30pm when we saw Dad". It must have been a huge relief to be re-united as a family in the midst of the disaster. How they got back to their temporary home at the Taradale Racecourse is a bit hazy, but Dawn recalls that when they arrived, they had neighbours. "More tents had been erected to accommodate hundreds of patients who had been injured in the earthquake, and the wood we had collected was a god send".   In the days that followed Dawn remembers sharing her bed so the nurses could have a sleep between their shifts. Roy's damaged bike was retrieved from the wreckage three weeks later as it had been buried during the earthquake. In hindsight it was a miracle that Dawn's family survived the disaster with a just a few scratches.

After the earthquake, nearly all of the buildings in Napier and Hastings were demolished. Many families became homeless within minutes and subsequently had to leave the region to seek refuge. Frighteningly, there were hundreds of aftershocks which went on for several years; some were felt as far afield as Wellington more than 320 kilometres away. Dawn remembers going back to their home in Ōtāne with her parents and seeing the wreckage, "all of the preserves had fallen off the shelves" –

it was an indescribable mess. Like hundreds of others, Dawn's family relocated from Taradale to Waipawa 90 kilometres away, where they lived in tents on the riverbed. Dawn went to school in Waipawa until she was seven years old. To give everyone a lift Dawn's grandparents brought their children and grandchildren together for a couple of weeks in Haumoana, a small coastal settlement in Hawkes Bay. When the holiday came to an end, Dawn's family stayed on in Haumoana and made this their home for the next ten years.

Dawn went to Haumoana Primary School and later caught the bus to attend high school in Hastings. All through school she took part in school concerts, drama and theatre as she thoroughly enjoyed entertaining others. As a gregarious ten-year-old, Dawn said, "I wrote a play and charged people one penny each to come and watch it"! At high school, she went to elocution lessons, entered lots of speech competitions and proudly revealed "I won a highly commended award for a Shakespearean competition and later won first prize for a Shakespearean speech competition in Wellington". Encouraged by her parents, Dawn basked in the performing arts.

In 1942 Dawn's parents relocated to Lower Hutt when her father secured construction work in the Wellington Region. Dawn was re-united with her parents when she left school a couple of months later. At 17 years of age, she got an office job at the Department of Scientific and Industrial Research (DSIR), which at the time was doing its bit for the war effort. Within a few short years Dawn quickly worked her way through the ranks and became the Head Typist. After leaving the DSIR she was appointed as Mr Murray Tingey's Secretary, a role she held for two years with R. and E. Tingey in Wellington.

During the lunch breaks several of the staff at the DSIR used to get together to play table tennis and sometimes they'd go dancing at the Rowing Club. Ken McCormick, a trainee electrician with the DSIR used to join in and bit by bit Dawn got to know Ken and his sister. Over time Ken and Dawn's relationship blossomed. The couple married in 1950 at St Stephen's Presbyterian Church in Lower Hutt.

Describing her husband Dawn said, "Ken was extremely clever and good with all things electrical including heating and ventilation. When he was 21 years old, he got a job at the Dunlop factory where he was in charge of all things electrical". The newlyweds bought a section in Trentham before they were married, and with the help of Dawn's Dad, they built a two-bedroomed home on it for the grand sum of 2,000 pounds. Dawn said, "Ken did all the electrical work on it himself". Their first child Gary was born in 1951, followed by Paul in 1952 and Mark in 1956.

The McCormick family used to go to Tītahi Bay for holidays where they spent their days on the beach swimming, went sledging and played table tennis. By this time, the family had outgrown their Hutt Valley home. They liked Tītahi Bay, Ken and Dawn decided to buy a section there and build a house on it. They sold their two-bedroomed home in the Hutt Valley, and while their new home was being built the family lived in a little seaside bach (traditionally a small holiday home). The children attended the local school, quickly made friends, enjoyed hiking and sledging in the surrounding area with their parents, and like most youngsters, pursued their own interests including music. Within a few years Dawn and Ken realised they needed more space. By this time their lads were teenagers and were bringing their friends home with them. Dawn and Ken looked for another property in Tītahi Bay that met their needs. They settled on a four bedroomed house that had a games room, a swimming pool, a garage and a big two-story workshop which was ideal for Ken's projects. It was perfect for entertaining all their guests.

Meanwhile, Dawn became heavily involved with Tītahi Bay Little Theatre, now Porirua Little Theatre. She loved it and said, "in 14 years I never saw a show from the front". Everyone in the McCormick family participated in the theatre productions in one way or another - acting, singing, dancing, making and playing instruments, building the scenery, the props and managing the lighting.

To help raise funds for the Little Theatre Dawn took responsibility for organising children's concerts. After promoting the idea to the community, hordes of children showed an interest, so she taught the children a variety of song and dance routines – in schools and with the Little Theatre. For the next three years Dawn organised a children's concert every year, each with its own theme. These concerts were hugely successful as the children loved performing on stage in their costumes for their families and friends, and sometimes their parents joined in!

In the 1960's and 70's there was limited entertainment in Tītahi Bay. Dawn used to take her mother and mother-in-law to the Friendship Club that used to meet socially at the Baptist Church. It was an opportunity for the older community to come together for a shared lunch and take part in various activities and games. Initially Dawn helped out with the lunches, welcomed people to the meetings and managed the sales table, and soon took responsibility for organising the entertainment. Finding it difficult to source singers, dancers, musicians etc., she initiated a skiffle troupe, and they provided the entertainment for the members. Dawn said, "it was so much fun, everyone loved it and there was always a good turnout at the monthly meetings".

Inspired by the reaction from the community, Dawn established her own performance troupe called 'The Golden Girls' with the support of like-minded friends. For the next 13 years the troupe got together every Monday afternoon to plan and rehearse their music hall variety shows. Dawn organised the music – re-introducing all of the old songs, organised the costumes, and performed with the troupe. Reminiscing Dawn said, "our performances were very slick; the timing was perfect".

The last show the Golden Girls performed under Dawn's direction was called 'Around the World', where all of the song and dance routines were performed in the national dress of the countries characterised in the songs. The troupe performed to delighted audiences all over the Wellington Region and as far north as the Horowhenua, "it was a huge commitment, but we had so much fun, and people really appreciated it". When

Dawn stepped back from the Little Theatre, the troupe continued to perform for several more years.

During this period Dawn became more involved with the Friendship Group, took on the role as President and remained a member for 35 years. She was also heavily involved in a huge project to restore the oldest Presbyterian church in Tītahi Bay. Dawn recalls, "this was a very rewarding community project. We not only spent time fundraising, but we also physically did much of the restoration work ourselves. It was hard work, but we were so proud of what we had achieved for our community".

One day a friend invited her to a painting exhibition that was held in a homestead in Pāuatahanui, and Dawn went along to keep her company. It turned out to be a 'hands on' event where participants had the opportunity to draw and paint. Dawn said, "I liked colouring in when I was child, but I'd never had any lessons on how to draw and paint". The activity sparked her interest and, at 70 years of age, ignited a form of expression she hadn't previously considered. Dawn enjoyed her newfound hobby and encouraged by her peers, she showed one of her paintings in a local exhibition. Ken hadn't taken her new hobby seriously and was astounded when she told him her painting of a cottage sold for $100. Developing her artistic talent throughout her 70's, 80's and into her 90's Dawn has created dozens of works of art that have been shown in exhibitions at Pātaka Art and Museum in Porirua, and galleries in Pāuatahanui and Whanganui. This talented artist has sold more than 60 paintings over the years, some of which have been taken overseas. One of Dawn's paintings of Tītahi Bay was purchased by Porirua City Council and hangs in the Council Chambers.

Over time Dawn and Ken's sons grew up, left home and had families of their own. Gary moved to the South Island, and Paul and Mark moved to Whanganui, while Ken and Dawn remained in the large family home in Tītahi Bay. When Paul opened a business in Whanganui, Dawn and Ken travelled up to join the family to celebrate the occasion. They really liked the city and although they had no plans to move at the time, they looked at a few properties to get the feel of the place. Quite by chance a lovely two-story house was on the market that had everything Dawn wanted in a home, and it had a big workshop – a feature that was extremely important to Ken. Captivated by the house they'd viewed it was the topic of conversation on the drive back to Tītahi Bay. The couple talked it over and decided that maybe it might not be a bad idea to sell their large home and move to Whanganui. After all, the district offered everything they wanted or needed, and they'd be closer to some of the family – but they would only move if they could purchase that particular house. They promptly made a bid on the Whanganui home and, when their offer was accepted, they sold their home in Tītahi Bay where they had lived for 33 years.

Dawn and Ken were aged 81 and 80 respectively when they moved into their new home in a leafy suburb in Whanganui. Dawn captured the street beautifully in one of the oil paintings that's displayed on the wall in her lounge. The couple settled into the community and enjoyed four happy years in their new home before Ken became ill. Ken was diagnosed with cancer. Dawn cared for him during his illness with support from family and friends. Regrettably, Ken died in 2011 aged 85. Dawn and Ken had been happily married for 61 years. Following Ken's funeral, Dawn initially decided to stay in the two-story home she and her husband had shared. As can be expected, there was a period of adjustment, but Dawn got on with her life. An independent woman, she organised a trip, booked motels and drove around the lower half of the North Island by herself – no mean feat when you are 89 years of age!

Dawn wisely didn't make any hasty decisions when Ken died. Eighteen months later she reconsidered her options as by this time her arthritis was getting worse. They had installed a chairlift for Ken, so she didn't have to manage the stairs, but she knew the house was too big for her and told herself, "Time to move Dawn". Knowing the area well she chose to move into a single level two-bedroomed villa in a retirement village, that is located in the same street she lived in at the time. It was a good decision, as she could maintain her connection with her interests, her friends and her family.   Dawn was 90 years old when she moved into her new home.

A year later, Dawn noticed her eyesight was deteriorating. She said, "It was getting harder to see when I was driving, so I rang my son up and told him to come and get the car – it's yours". The decision to give up your driver's licence is always a difficult one but staying safe on the road is the number one priority and, for most people, there are alternative means of transport. Despite difficulties with her eyesight Dawn continued to paint until she was 94 years old and then took up felting. Now she goes to art classes every Tuesday afternoon where she makes decorative felt and leather purses and lambswool cushions with likeminded artists. She was recently made an honorary member of the Whanganui Arts Society – the highest distinction that a club can bestow for meritorious service. Within days of receiving the news Dawn sold two of her paintings.

Whilst some physical aspects of ageing are inevitable, Dawn's approach to life demonstrates that our chronological age is just a number, mindset matters. At 96 years of age, she values her autonomy, is very self-sufficient, does her own housekeeping, bakes regularly, and she clearly demonstrates that it's never too late to learn something new. A very social person Dawn, who is also fondly known as 'Mrs Mc' by some members of the community, loves life and makes the most of it.

A loving Mum, grandmother, and great grandmother she is very proud of her three sons who are all very successful - Gary McCormick is a Radio Broadcaster in the South Island, Paul McCormick is a retired Chiropractor living in South Carolina, and Mark McCormick manages a business in Whanganui. She has seven granddaughters, two grandsons, and two great grandsons.

Dawn and Ken

Dawn's 21st Birthday

Dawn on her Wedding Day

Dawn in costume

Dressed for a show at Titahi Bay.
Paul McCormick, second from the front. Gary is fourth from the front.

Dawn's painting of the street where she lives in Whanganui.

'Taranaki Melting Snow'.

Dawn and Ken's 60th Wedding Anniversary

Dawn McCormick - 'Mrs Mc'

Dawn and Ken with their three sons

KATH TURKINGTON

Kath, the second of two children, was born in Portsmouth, England in August 1920. This year she celebrates her 100th birthday. As the last remaining member of her generation of the Norgate and Turkington families, she appreciates that becoming a centenarian is a real achievement and a huge milestone. Kath has so many memories of her own personal journey, the special people she has shared it with, and the context in which her experiences have taken shape. Reflecting on her life she said, "I have been blessed in life with a special parentage, a wonderful husband, a loving, caring family, a special companion and many, many loving friends. It's a long life - a life full of the knowledge of a loving heavenly Father".

Twelve years ago, Kath belonged to a group of about ten people from her church who met regularly to write and share their stories with one another. Over time, Kath has documented quite a collection of her memories. This is a very special gift for her beloved family – her two sons, nine grandchildren, nine great grandchildren, her nieces and nephews, and her friends. It's a pleasure to share a snapshot of Kath's life with you too.

One of her earliest memories is as a three-year-old when she and her family came to New Zealand as assisted migrants on the ship 'Rotorua'. Kath distinctly remembers the fancy-dress party on the voyage. Her mother had dressed her as a bon-bon in mauve crepe paper, and much to her embarrassment, the elastic broke in her knickers, and they kept falling down!

In New Zealand, the family settled in Wellington. Kath's father, Frank Norgate, was a carpenter with Fletcher Construction Company. Daisy, Kath's mother was a qualified seamstress, and regularly took on sewing to support the family's income. Kath and her older brother Ronald went to Brooklyn School, just a few minutes' walk from their home.

Sundays were sacred days for Kath's family who went to Christian Endeavour at 10am, and church at 11am. In the afternoon Kath and her brother joined their father who taught Sunday school at the Mornington Baptist Church. A highlight for the children were the Sunday School picnics whereby families travelled on the tram together to Seatoun and congregated at the beach. Kath said these picnics were great fun. Children's races were held in the morning, and then, "everyone sat in a circle while the teachers handed round the sandwiches, a piece of fruit cake or a bun, and always an apple".

Growing up in the 1920's and 30's was quite a challenge. Kath, who had peritonitis when she was nine years old, vividly remembers the midnight ambulance trip to Abel Smith Street private hospital for an operation followed by three weeks recuperation. Luckily, she made a good recovery, but her parents had to take out an extra mortgage to pay the bill! Despite the trauma Kath did well at primary school. After achieving her 'Proficiency' certificate' aged 12, she went to Wellington Technical College where she completed a commercial course and passed the "Junior Public Service examination in shorthand and typing (80 words per minute in shorthand and 40 words per minute in typing)". Kath's schooling occurred during the 'Great Depression' – a time when there were few jobs, high unemployment and families struggled to afford the cost of books and uniforms. Kath's mother made her uniform, "a brown-flannel tunic – when everyone else had serge" and she recalls "the humiliation of having to line up at the school office each week to pay for my books on the installment system as everyone knew you were poor!"

During the Great Depression, Kath's father, like thousands of others, lost his job. Kath remembers "how soul-destroying it was for him as he walked the streets looking for work. He had cardboard in his shoes as the soles were worn out". Her father set up a soup kitchen at their church, where he boiled up meat bones in a big copper fueled with the wood, he'd chopped to feed the fire. Fortuitously, her father managed to secure "relief work" developing the road that went to Mount Crawford Prison, and "was able to defer the mortgage payments until he had regular employment". Things improved for the family when her father got a job preparing the site to build Wellington's new railway station. Kath clearly remembers the family going to 'The Ritz' for tea to celebrate the occasion and recalls "having salmon mayonnaise – the most delicious meal I had ever tasted".

In her teens, Kath went to Bible Class camps and joined the Girls' Life Brigade where she, "learned skills that stood me in good stead throughout my life". She has fond memories of the fun times they had taking part in the Wellington area competitions and camping expeditions. When Kath's family moved to Plimmerton, she assisted with the local Girls Brigade company for several years.

During the school holidays, Kath's family rented a bach in Pukerua Bay. Kath recalls packing their cases "with gusto" and the family, along with the dog, caught the steam train to Pukerua Bay. A 'bach' is traditionally a small and very modest family holiday or beach home, and as such, is an iconic past of New Zealand's culture and heritage. The Pukerua Bay bach had no running water, so Kath and Ronald used to get it "from a tap at the bottom of the hill". They also collected driftwood to light the fire for cooking. These carefree holidays were such fun as the days were spent "watching all the activity in rockpools, making sandcastles, going for swims, walking the dog and generally enjoying all the Bay had to offer".

In the year she turned 15, Kath secured her first job, a temporary secretarial role. After passing an entrance examination, she began her career as a shorthand typist in the Railways Department. During the war years (1939-44), she was seconded to help form the 'Food and Rationing Control Office' – the office responsible for the provisions for the Armed Forces, American transit camps and all of the government institutions (e.g., prisons, canteens, camps, railway refreshment rooms and health areas). As Wellington experienced many earthquakes during the war, Kath recalls "it was a shaky existence, and I spent a good deal of time under my desk" – this workplace was built on reclaimed land!

In 1940, the Centennial Exhibition was built in Kilbirnie in Wellington to commemorate the 100th anniversary of the signing of the Treaty of Waitangi and 100th anniversary of New Zealand's membership of the British Empire. Kath said, "the whole country was planning to make this a great success and a place to be proud of". The exhibition was indeed "spectacular". Spread over 55 acres of land, the building contained an infinite number of trade and tourist attractions, as well as fun attractions such as a "roller coaster and a ghost house". These displays were "surrounded by impressive water displays and fancy lighting". At the time, the British warship 'Ramillies' was docked in Wellington Harbour, and the crew were granted free admission to the exhibition. As luck would have it, Kath and her friend met a couple of the crew at a church service, and they invited their new friends to join them at the exhibition. Kath recalls "it was an amazing experience and so much fun, so much so we missed the last tram and had to walk home".

During the war, Kath's family were approached to take in a boarder. Colin Christie, a 17-year-old trainee telegraphist with the Post Office from Whangārei, came to live with the family and he and Kath became quite friendly. Colin was also in the Territorials, and, like many young men, he was called up to serve. He was posted to Norfolk Island for meteorological observations and, with the threat of the Japanese expansion into the South Pacific, his work included coast watching. Although the couple corresponded by letter every other day, these were trying times and inevitably the relationship ended.

After the war, when the Food and Rationing Control Office was disbanded, Kath went back to work in Head Office in the typist's room where she met Doreen Turkington. Doreen introduced her to her brother Mervyn, who had just finished his first year at the Bible Training

Institute in Auckland and was home for the Christmas holidays. The next day Merv rang Kath at work and invited her out for lunch. The friendship progressed, and within a month Mervyn popped the question. Kath said, "it was love at first sight. I had no hesitation in saying yes". Mervyn didn't return to the Bible Training Institute. Instead, he settled in Tawa and completed his Plumbing and Drain laying apprenticeship. After saving for two years, Mervyn and Kath were married on 18th December 1948 at the Brooklyn Baptist Church.

After the wedding Kath left the Railways Dept., as, "in those days, marriage for women was your career". Kath's parents shared their home with the newlyweds, enabling Kath to care for them both as their health deteriorated. A few years later, Kath and Mervyn bought the family home when they won a 'draw' with their Building Society. Mervyn and his brother went on to form their own business, "Turkington Bros", servicing clients in the Plimmerton, Porirua and Tawa area. Their business truck was used for their family's camping holidays.

Kath and Mervyn were happily married for 48 years and were blessed with two children, John, and Bruce. As a family they were involved with the Methodist church and started a Sunday School in Motuhara Road. As a local preacher, Mervyn often took services in the Plimmerton, Paremata, Porirua and Elsdon areas. Kath became involved with the Methodist Women's Missionary Union, (later known as the Methodist Women's Fellowship). She served on the Wellington District Executive and was their

President for a two-year period. Kath was a member of the Wellington Branch of the National Council of Women, where she was the Secretary for two years. She was also a member of the Council of Wellington Churches and various other organisations connected to the Methodist Church. In this capacity she attended numerous Church conferences and conventions. Reflecting back on these days Kath said, "what little contribution I have made has been multiplied for me by the friendships made, and the knowledge that nothing can separate me from God's love and care".

When the Turkington brothers retired in 1982, Kath and Mervyn took the opportunity to return to Kath's birthplace in Britain and meet up with family and friends. It was "a very exciting time" for the couple to go back to their roots and they "thoroughly enjoyed" their three month vacation, even though many of the landmarks they had heard about no longer existed in post-war Britain.

Sadly, in 1996, Mervyn died on the couple's wedding anniversary, after battling cancer for quite a few years. Kath still has the card she took to the hospital to share with him. After his death Kath said her "life seemed to stand still". By this time both of her sons were married with families of their own. Kath had a big section to care for, the home needed maintenance and she concluded that "I needed to take myself in hand and make provision for an advancing older age". Kath made a courageous decision and bought a home in a retirement village on the Kāpiti Coast where she could re-establish herself, make new friends and have fewer money worries as the rates were included in her monthly fee. Kath said, "it was quite a wrench" to sell the home she had lived in for 53 years and move to another community, but she knew she had made the right decision when she realized, "God is always with me wherever my house is".

In 2002, out of the blue, Kath received a surprise telephone call from her old friend Colin Christie. As previously mentioned, the war years had separated Kath and Colin from one another in their youth. At the time Colin was living in a retirement village in Whangārei and as he too was on his own, Kath and he decided to renew the relationship. Things progressed from that first telephone call. Initially Kath and Colin corresponded with one another. Later they made the decision to live together in Kāpiti. "These years together were ones of great companionship and joy, and we were able to do fun things together," said Kath. The couple jointly participated in various activities with their families and friends, travelled extensively in New Zealand and took a trip to Australia. They enjoyed six happy years together before Colin died suddenly, very peacefully, in his sleep in 2009.

It was around this time that Kath met with a group of people at her church to write short stories and share them with one another. When someone suggested they share a memory about a family member Kath saw it as an ideal opportunity to pay a tribute to her much loved and respected father who died when she lived in Plimmerton. Over time Kath captured many memories about her life and the special people who have played a part in it. Through the decades, she has seen so many changes take place. Reflecting on the past is a very thought provoking and empowering experience and helps to clarify who we are and what's important to us. Looking back Kath has realized how blessed she has been in life.

At 96 years of age Kath made the decision to give up driving her car and handed in her driving license. Over the next 12 months she missed the independence her own transport had given her and began to feel a bit isolated living in her house on the hill in Kāpiti Village. At 97 years of age, she decided to sell her house and move to a large, serviced apartment in another retirement village that was in close proximity to the main shopping area as well as all the amenities she had been accustomed to, for example, a shopping bus, laundry facilities, and plenty of social activities. In her new home her midday meals are provided in a lovely restaurant and her apartment is cleaned once a week. Kath said, "it was a big decision – but a good one". Since moving to her new home, she has joined the fortnightly 'Musical Appreciation' group and attends the weekly 'Steady as you go' exercise class, (Kath can get out of her chair without assistance – not bad at 99 years of age). She is a member of the scrabble group, attends the village meetings and forums, and likes to have her regular 'shampoo and set' at the hairdressers. Kath enjoys the 'Daytime Operatunity Concerts', is a member of Kāpiti Uniting Church and keeps in touch with her family and friends.

Kath especially enjoys time with her two sons, her grandchildren, great grandchildren and her nieces and nephews. She sees them whenever she can, and they have celebrated lots of family occasions together. The whole family spent the weekend at the Anglican Family Camp in Ōtaki for Kath's 90th birthday where more than 100 people joined them for the celebration. Kath celebrated her 95th birthday party at Kāpiti Village, and her 99th birthday party was held at Kāpiti Uniting Church in Raumati.

She has thoroughly enjoyed these wonderful celebrations, and whilst there is a photo board on display, she found there was little time to chat with everyone present and explain who everyone is. Approaching her 100th birthday Kath collated and published her memories and gifted a copy to all of her family and friends who came along to help her celebrate this momentous occasion. It's a precious gift few families have and will be truly treasured. As Steve Saint once said:-

"Your story is the greatest legacy that you will leave to your friends. It's the longest-lasting legacy you will leave to your heirs".

Kath with her parents at their home in Brooklyn in1924

Kath and her brother Ronald with their Mother.

Church Parade Brooklyn 1933-34

Kath at the1940 Exhibition Show in Kilbirnie

Kath and Mervyn's Wedding Day, 1948

The Turkington's truck

Colin and Kath in their villa

Kath celebrating her 95th Birthday with her sons John and Bruce.

Kath celebrating her 99th Birthday with members of the Norgate and
Turkington families

AFTERTHOUGHTS

A huge debt of gratitude is due to the awesome individuals who generously shared their stories with me. It's with their permission that a lifetime of wildly different backgrounds, experiences and perspectives can be shared with you. While each of the life stories are unique, they share some common threads. In the second half of life all of these individuals have chosen to live in New Zealand for at least part of the year. Ranging in age from their mid-50's to 100, some are single, have partners, are married or are widowed – just like us. Whilst the physiological aspects of ageing varied from person to person, these men and women choose to proactively pursue activities that interest them ensuring they maintain their physical and mental health and wellbeing. Contrary to popular belief, these individuals demonstrate that frailty and ill-health are not inevitable in the latter decades of our lives.

Everyone's life is unique, and we all experience the highs and lows along the journey – both the uplifting, joyful experiences, and distressingly painful times. Despite the unique set of circumstances and challenges these men and women have encountered, they appreciate that their experiences, and the lessons they have learned along the way, have shaped who they are and the choices they make. They are resilient. Their attitudes to life and their perspective on ageing is both insightful and inspirational. They embrace life and all that it offers on their own terms, and as they look towards the future, they continue to flourish in later life. Inspired by their example, whatever our age and circumstances, so can we!

It's been an honour to have met these individuals, and a privilege to be able to share their stories with you. I hope you have enjoyed them. With our extended lifespans, chronological age becomes less and less relevant. Life is a continuous adventure. As such, it's never too late to change direction, start something new, live in a different place, make bold decisions, take on significant projects and invest in meaningful relationships. Let's make the most of our extended lifespans. After all, life truly is a gift for us to enjoy, and later life can be even more fulfilling than what has gone before. I'll leave you with wise words from Marty Rubin,

"Everything is irrelevant but this:

To embrace life.

To feel it.

To savour it.

To love it"

THANK YOU

Thank you for reading **Embracing Life On Our Own Terms**. I hope you enjoyed it. I'd really appreciate it if you would take a few minutes to provide a review of this book, whether positive or negative as reviews help other readers find books that would be of interest to them.

By the same author

 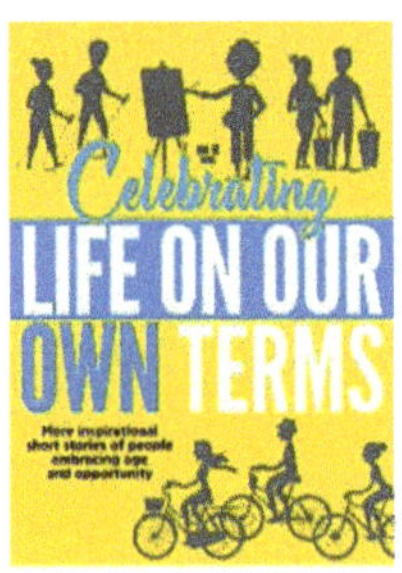

Available online from your favourite bookstores

Coming soon
Creating Life On Our Own Terms
and
Entrepreneurs @ 50+ - Yes, We Can!

Want to be kept up-to-date with new books and news?

If so, email me to register your interest and be one of the first to find out when new books are released.

kiaora@angelarobertson.nz

ABOUT THE AUTHOR

Dr Angela Robertson has over 30 years' experience as a professional learning and development practitioner, manager, coach, writer and speaker. She inspires and supports individuals of all ages to maximise their potential to enhance the quality of their lives, work and relationships.

Angela lives with her husband Bill on the beautiful Kāpiti Coast in New Zealand.